100% UNOFFICIAL

100% UNOFFICIAL

100% UNOFFICIAL

100% UNOFFICIAL

100% UNOFFICIAL

100%
UNOFFICIAL

First published in Great Britain 2026 by 100% Unofficial, a part of Farshore
An imprint of HarperCollins*Publishers*
1 London Bridge Street, London SE1 9GF
www.farshore.co.uk

HarperCollins*Publishers*
Macken House, 39/40 Mayor Street Upper,
Dublin 1, D01 C9W8, Ireland

Written by Malcolm Croft

This book is an original creation by Farshore

ISBN 978 00 0 883620 7
Printed in Romania
001

A CIP catalogue record for this title is available from the British Library.

100% UNOFFICIAL

Harry Styles Annual 2027

100% UNOFFICIAL

Contents

Keep Calm and Harry On!

Harry's back! After a three-year musical absence, the Golden Boy has returned – and his fans couldn't be happier. Of course, he never really went away. He was just busy living his best life, so he had loads to tell us about when he came back ...

DID YOU MISS HIM?

Harry's return with *Kiss All the Time. Disco, Occasionally.* sparked global mania when it was announced on 15 January, 2026. Fans eagerly began counting down the days! From his cheeky, feel-good fan interactions and flamboyant stage outfits to his fruit-themed songs and wonderfully weird music videos – and that famous smile, of course – everyone has their own favourite Harry moment they look forward to seeing again. So, the big question is: what did YOU miss most about Harry?

No worries, darling! Harry in Venice.

LA DOLCE VITA

After *Love On Tour* ended in 2023 – famously in Reggio Emilia, Italy, as you'll discover – Harry took a deliberate break to focus on his private life and happiness. He returned to Italy, his new favourite place in the world, after falling in love with the Amalfi Coast while filming the **'Golden'** video in 2020, and spending lots of time there in 2024. "Italy has become really special to me," he has said. "When I was in Rome, the city taught me how to slow down. The Romans are the best at that – it's their speciality." Italians even have a famous philosophy called la dolce vita, meaning 'the sweet life', all about enjoying simple pleasures and taking their time. They also say 'piano piano' – 'slowly, slowly' – as a reminder there's no need to hurry. Harry can even speak Italian now. Ciao!

HARRY FINDS HAPPINESS (?)

As the whole world knows, Harry has been linked to quite a few famous girlfriends. We don't have space here to name them all – just joking, Harry! Right now, he's rumoured to be loved up with actor Zoë Kravitz, best known as Catwoman in 2022's *The Batman*. The pair have been spotted on several dates in London and New York. Harry even seems to have the approval of Zoë's famous rock-star dad, Lenny Kravitz.

WE BELONG TOGETHER

To reveal his fourth studio album, *Kiss All the Time. Disco, Occasionally.*, Harry launched a cryptic global teaser that got fans guessing. On 12 January, posters reading "WE BELONG TOGETHER" appeared in cities around the world, sending fans not only into a frenzy but also to a website that redirected them to a WhatsApp group. A few days later, a voice note of Harry softly mumbling the phrase was sent to fans! On 15 January, he officially announced the album, new single **'Aperture'** and a world tour. The news BROKE THE INTERNET!

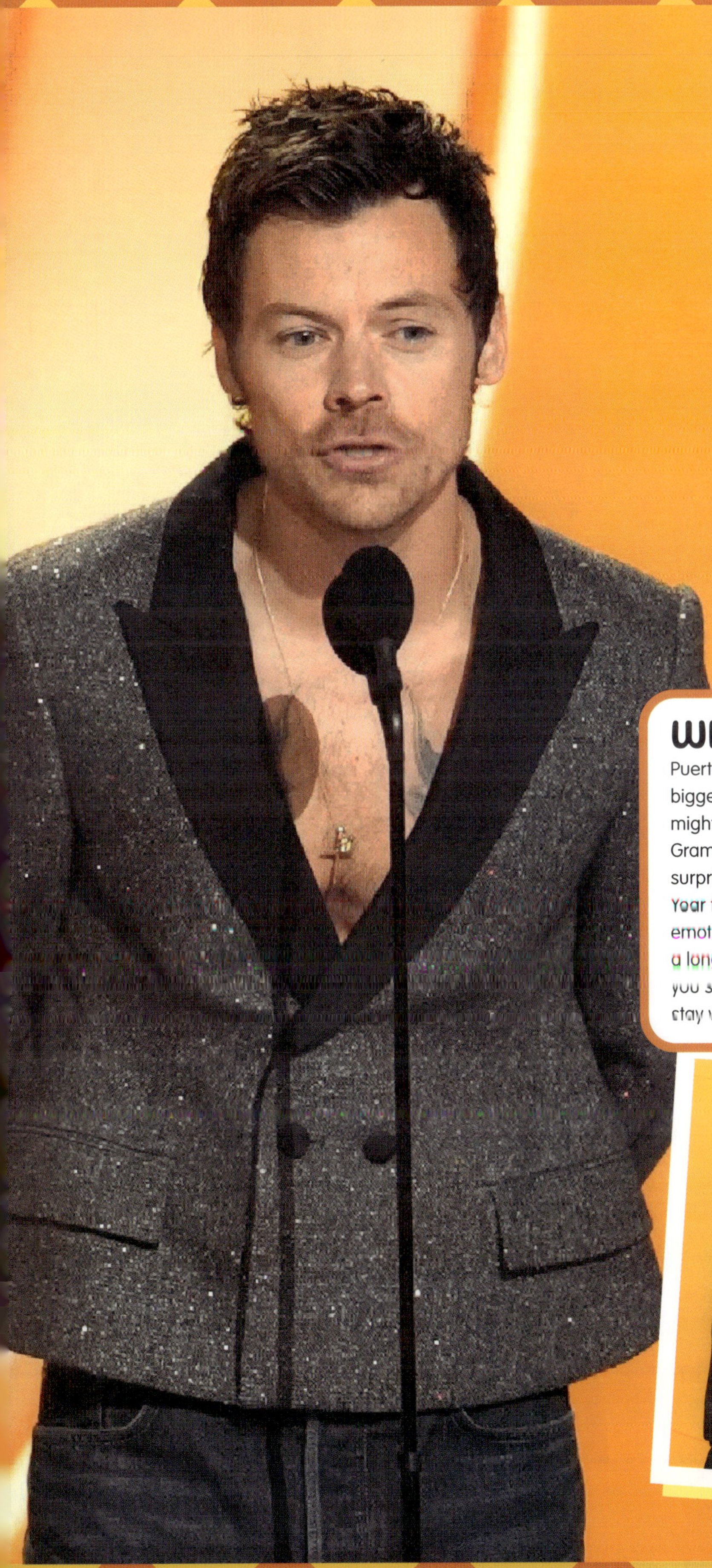

> For a really long time, I was terrified of what my life was if I wasn't making music. So, I stopped for a second and thought, 'What does it actually mean to make something? And what does it mean to me to make something as my job?'

Harry on slowing down.

WHEN HARRY MET BUNNY

Puerto Rican pop star Bad Bunny is, without a doubt, the biggest artist in the world right now – although Harry's return might shake things up! The pair met for the first time at the Grammy Awards in February 2026, when Harry made a surprise appearance to present Bad Bunny with Album of the Year for *Debí Tirar Más Fotos*. The right man for the job! The emotional moment left Bunny visibly tearful and the two shared a long hug on stage. "A truly great album can change the way you see everything," Harry said on the night. "The best albums stay with you – you can return to them like old friends."

Harry passes the pop icon baton to Bunny.

Story of His Life

Since his stylish arrival in 2010, Harry's fans have watched the singing superstar soar to truly stratospheric heights. From working in a bakery to performing at sold-out stadiums, it's been an incredible journey. So, the big question is: where were YOU when Harry was here? ...

Dressed to impress, even then!

1994 → 2010 → 2011 → 2012 → 2015 → 2016 →

1 FEBRUARY 1994
Harry Edward Styles is born in Redditch, Worcestershire, UK – on a Tuesday afternoon, FYI!

11 APRIL 2010
Encouraged by his mother, Harry auditions for *The X Factor* in Manchester as a solo contestant, singing Train's **'Hey, Soul Sister'**.

23 JULY 2010
Harry's first televised *The X Factor* audition airs. He sang Stevie Wonder's **'Isn't She Lovely'**.

9 OCTOBER 2010
One Direction perform live for the first time on *The X Factor* finals.

11 DECEMBER 2010
One Direction finish third in *The X Factor* final but secure a major record deal.

11 SEPTEMBER 2011
1D debut single **'What Makes You Beautiful'** is released and becomes a global smash hit!

20 MARCH 2012
1D album *Up All Night* is released in the US and debuts at No. 1 on the US Billboard 200 chart!

25 MARCH 2015
Zayn Malik leaves One Direction in the middle of their *On The Road Again* Tour. Fans are shocked.

23 AUGUST 2015
1D announce an indefinite hiatus starting in 2016 to focus on solo projects.

7 DECEMBER 2016
Harry is announced as part of the cast of Christopher Nolan's epic World War II film, *Dunkirk*.

7 APRIL 2017
'Sign of the Times', Harry's debut solo single, is released to critical acclaim.

12 MAY 2017
Harry's self-titled debut solo album *Harry Styles* is released.

19 SEPTEMBER 2017
Harry begins his first solo world tour at The Masonic in San Francisco, USA.

15 MARCH 2021
Harry wins his first Grammy Award for Best Pop Solo Performance for **'Watermelon Sugar'**.

18 MAY 2021
He wins the BRIT Award for Best British Single for **'Watermelon Sugar'**.

5 FEBRUARY 2023
OMG! *Harry's House* wins the Grammy Award for Album of the Year.

24 FEBRUARY 2023
Harry wins four BRIT Awards, including: Artist of the Year and Album of the Year for *Harry's House*.

22 JULY 2023
The final show of *Love On Tour* takes place in Reggio Emilia, Italy, closing a historic global tour.

23 JANUARY 2026
Harry returns! He releases lead single **'Aperture'** from his new album.

6 MARCH 2026
Harry Styles' long-awatied fourth studio album, *Kiss All The Time. Disco, Occasionally*, is released.

16 MAY 2026
The *Together, Together* tour starts at the Johan Cruyff Arena in Amsterdam, The Netherlands.

2017 → 2019 → 2021 → 2022 → 2023 → 2026

16 NOVEMBER 2019
He is both host and musical guest on *Saturday Night Live*, singing **'Lights Up'** and **'Watermelon Sugar'**.

13 DECEMBER 2019
Fine Line debuts at No. 1 on the US chart with the biggest first-week sales by an English male artist.

1 APRIL 2022
'As It Was', the lead single from *Harry's House*, is released, quickly becoming a worldwide sensation!

20 MAY 2022
Third studio album *Harry's House* is released – nothing is ever the same as it was.

29 OCTOBER 2022
Harry becomes the first member of One Direction to headline California's *Coachella Festival*.

"Everything in my life has felt like a bonus since *The X Factor*."

Harry on his amazing career – so far!

Take Me Home

Fancy a trip down Memory Lane to the place – and time – where Harry's story first began? Alright then ... next stop: sleepy Holmes Chapel, Cheshire!

Son shines! Harry loves his mum, Anne.

HOMETOWN GLORY

Before Harry-mania and *The X Factor*, Harry lived a very humble life in Holmes Chapel, Cheshire – a village located between Manchester and Stoke-on-Trent that dates back to 1430. Today, it's still quite small with a population of just 6,000. It was in this picturesque place that Harry played his first gig, landed his first job and attended Holmes Chapel Comprehensive School. "It's quite boring and nothing much ever happens there," Harry said in his 2010 *The X Factor* audition. Even today, Holmes Chapel is the place where Harry returns home to "disappear". "I go back to Cheshire and walk around the same fields and it's one of the things that isn't going to change, no matter what happens," he has said.

ABOVE A PUB

Before his mum, Anne, and dad, Desmond, divorced in 2001, Harry lived above the Antrobus Arms pub in Northwich, Cheshire with his beloved sister, Gemma, and a pet hamster (called Hamster!). "I could always hear my sister's music at the top of the stairs, and I used to pretend to have a guitar and perform in the mirror in my bedroom," Harry has said of his earliest singing days. The pub gave him his first taste of live music too, with bands playing downstairs – noise that became so comforting he could fall asleep to it!

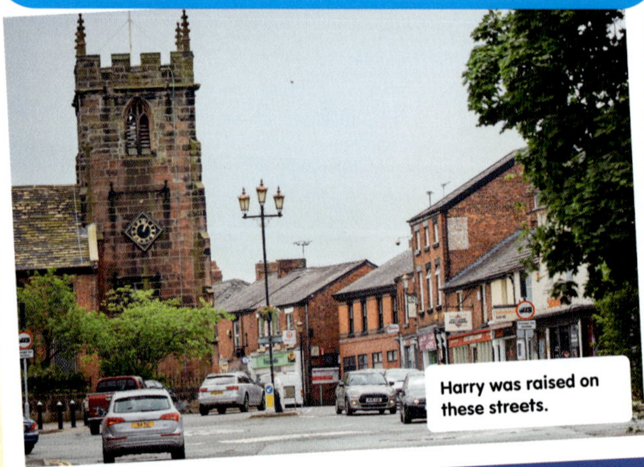

Harry was raised on these streets.

WHITE ESKIMO

One Direction weren't Harry's first band – White Eskimo were! The four-piece band, with Harry as lead singer, even won their school's Battle of the Bands and wrote original songs. One, **'Gone in a Week'**, was hilariously about luggage. During his 2010 *The X Factor* audition, Harry told viewers that performing with the band made him realise singing on stage was exactly what he wanted to do. Their first gig was a wedding, where they played cover songs such as **'Are You Gonna Be My Girl'** by Jet and **'Summer of '69'** by Bryan Adams. Don't believe it? Check out their 2010 videos on YouTube!

"Harry the little boy was boisterous. He didn't find it difficult to make friends and had his first girlfriend at the age of four or five. He would do what he wanted but often it seemed that what he wanted was to make other people happy."

Gemma Styles, on her brother.

SIX POUNDS AN HOUR

Harry's first job – famously revealed in the 2013 *One Direction: This Is Us* documentary – was as a shop assistant at the W. Mandeville bakery in Holmes Chapel. He earned £6 an hour; a tiny amount compared with the millions he can make from a single concert today. Harry joked that one perk of the job was getting "a nice bun on his break".

NEARLY A LAWYER

Before finding fame on *The X Factor*, Harry once considered a very different career: law. As a teenager, he thought about becoming a solicitor, which does sound a bit too boring for Harry. "I wanted to be a physiotherapist and then all my teachers told me, 'No jobs in that'. So I decided I wanted to be a lawyer," he revealed when he was 16. "This happened before I realised how hard you have to work to be a lawyer!" he said.

STAR PUPIL

Even at primary school, Harry was seen as a star pupil. His teacher, Mrs Vernon, said that although he was a very "cheeky" boy, "there was something special – a sparkle, a twinkle in his eye." He loved school, especially music and performing, and almost immediately after finishing his GCSEs he auditioned for *The X Factor* – the rest is history! "Listen to your teachers," he later said. "Every teacher has an important lesson to teach – some of which will last a lifetime."

FANCY A GUIDED TOUR?

In June 2024, organisers in Holmes Chapel launched a 2.5-hour guided walking tour of Harry's old stomping grounds. Stops include the bakery where he worked and the Tremlow Viaduct, featured in *One Direction: This Is Us*, where Harry famously signed his name. After 5,000 fans visited in 2023, officials had to recruit guides – with more than 150 superfans applying. Applicants even had to pass a tough 80-question quiz about Harry's life. Superfan Izzy Boughey got one of the lucky spots and now volunteers to show visitors around.

Imagine being served fresh bread by Harry!

> I had a really nice upbringing. I feel very lucky. I had a great family and always felt loved. There's nothing worse than an inauthentic tortured person.

Harry on his childhood.

Harry's Heroes

Like most modern artists, Harry draws inspiration from all kinds of places, from his mum Anne and sister Gemma to world-famous fashion designers and legendary performers. These influences haven't just helped shape the man he is today; they also represent the kind of artist he hopes to become in the years ahead ...

> "The people that I looked up to in music – Prince and David Bowie and Elvis and Freddie Mercury and Elton John – they're such showmen. As a kid they were completely mind-blowing."
>
> **Harry on his influences as inspiration.**

DAVID BOWIE

Often called 'the new Bowie', Harry has long been inspired by David Bowie, the fearless 1970s icon behind glam rock, **'Heroes'** and constant musical and fashion reinvention. Fans noticed the influence early on, with his debut solo single **'Sign of the Times'** compared to Bowie's dramatic style. Harry even travelled to Berlin – just as Bowie famously did – while recording *Kiss All The Time. Disco, Occasionally*. "Bowie can do no wrong," Harry said of his muse. Sadly, the two never met, as Bowie died in 2016. Imagine if they did – what a collab that would've been!

David Bowie in his Ziggy Stardust era.

PAUL McCARTNEY & WINGS

Harry has long admired Beatles legend Paul McCartney, calling him "one of the greatest songwriters of all time." McCartney's 1971 album *Ram* was on repeat while Harry made *Harry's House*, alongside Wings records like *London Town* and *Back to the Egg*. Seeing McCartney perform live in 2020 cemented Harry's ambitions as an artist. "Who ultimately do you want to be at the end of the day?" Harry Styles said. "You don't want to be the guy who died. You don't want to be the guy who's whacked out on drugs. You want to be the guy who's 80 and playing for three hours because he can and he wants to and everyone's loving it and he's having fun. I found it super inspiring. He's incredible."

JONI MITCHELL

Joni Mitchell's 1971 classic album *Blue* had a huge impact on Harry, both in childhood and later while making his solo music, inspiring intimate songs such as **'Matilda'**, **'Love Of My Life'** and **'Boyfriends'** – his legendary acoustic song sung in one take! "I was in a big Joni hole," he said during the making of *Fine Line*. He was so obsessed, he even tracked down the woman who built Joni's dulcimers (a traditional string instrument) in the 1960s, Joellen Lapidus, and took a lesson. Joellen made the dulcimer he plays on **'Canyon Moon'**.

Stevie Nicks with her (unofficially) adopted popstar son!

STEVIE NICKS

Harry shares a special bond with Fleetwood Mac legend Stevie Nicks. She even calls him her "little muse"! They first performed together in 2017, when she surprised fans at his now-legendary show at The Troubadour in LA. The pair first sang her song **'Landslide'** at the soundcheck in the empty venue and duetted on **'Two Ghosts'** in the show. In 2019, he inducted her into the Rock and Roll Hall of Fame, saying: "She is a beacon to all of us. Whenever you hear her voice, life gets just a little bit better. She's everything you've ever wanted in a lady, in a lover, and in a friend. Stephanie Nicks, I love you, we all do."

VAN MORRISON

Van Morrison is another musical hero Harry holds in the highest regard, especially the Irish legend's 1968 masterpiece *Astral Weeks*, praising its haunting folk sound and emotional songwriting. "It's my favourite album ever," Styles has said. "Completely perfect." He once posed for a backstage photo with Morrison and joked that he managed to make the infamously grumpy singer smile. Harry even played Morrison's epic nine-minute song **'Madame George'** before the start of his shows on his first solo tour in 2017, *Live On Tour*.

ELVIS PRESLEY

American icon of the 1950s, famous for **'Blue Suede Shoes'** and **'Heartbreak Hotel'**, Elvis Presley was one of Harry's very first musical heroes. Growing up, he was surrounded by the Elvis songs that were played by his family – it was the first music he ever heard, in fact – and loved singing them, especially **'The Girl of My Best Friend'**, the first song he recorded at home. "When I was little, we got a karaoke machine and I sang Elvis, because that's what my grandparents listened to. I made my grandfather a tape of me doing Elvis songs on one side and all Eminem on the other side. Unfortunately, I accidentally played him the wrong side." Hilarious!

Harry's probably thinking about buns and croissants!

> "I'm Harry Styles. I'm sixteen and I'm from Holmes Chapel in Cheshire."

Harry's first ever words on TV!

Isn't He Lovely

Long before Harry first burst into our lives and television screens on the UK's *The X Factor*, he already had that special something – the 'X factor' itself (even Rihanna later called him a "natural superstar"). It doesn't bear thinking about that without the singing show, the world might never have discovered his talent ...

THANK YOU MS TWIST!

Harry's mum knew her son belonged on stage when he was two or three years old – he was constantly singing around the house! When a customer at the bakery where he worked suggested entering a talent show, Harry wasn't so sure (he was too shy!) – Anne took the initiative and applied for *The X Factor.* "I went on the show because my Mum told me I was good ... but your Mum tells you things to make you feel good, so you take it with a pinch of salt!" Thankfully, he agreed to sing – and the rest is pop history!

THE FIRST AUDITION

On 11 April, 2010, Harry auditioned as a solo contestant for the seventh series of *The X Factor*, Britain's biggest TV show at the time, watched by nearly 20 million people each Saturday night. For his initial audition for the producers, he sang Train's **'Hey, Soul Sister'**, but after judge Simon Cowell suggested it didn't suit him, Harry switched to Stevie Wonder's classic **'Isn't She Lovely'** for his televised audition – and millions instantly fell in love with him. This performance was the beginning of his singing career

Harry was paid £30 a day as an *X Factor* auditionee.

With *The X Factor* creator, Simon Cowell.

HARRY NAMES THE BAND

It was Harry's idea to name the band One Direction after the boys were put together in the Groups category on *The X Factor*. As all the five members threw around suggestions, Harry proposed the name One Direction – and it stuck! "I suggested One Direction, and everyone was like, 'Yeah we like that,' and that was it. I thought it sounded good." Other ideas included Niall & The Potatoes (suggested by Niall as a joke!) and USP – Unique Selling Point – proposed by Liam's dad. In 2012, the band faced a legal challenge from a US group with the same name, but they kept it after the other band rebranded.

Niall with his 1D bro – Little Harry.

THANKS, NICOLE!

If anyone deserves credit for helping create One Direction, it might just be guest judge Nicole Scherzinger of the Pussycat Dolls. When Harry didn't make it past Boot Camp – along with Niall Horan, Zayn Malik, Louis Tomlinson and Liam Payne – she suggested to Simon Cowell that they would be "stronger as a group." She was spot on! The newly formed band reached the top three final contestants before they were eliminated. Matt Cardle went on to win.

BAND OF BROTHERS

They may have been put together by a complete stranger, but call it destiny – One Direction were meant to be! For five years, the boys experienced a level of fame not seen since Beatlemania in the 1960s. What helped them survive it was their beautiful brotherly bond with each other. "I look at artists who went through some version of what One Direction went through but on their own," Harry has said. "I can't imagine having done that. I feel really lucky that we always had each other."

"We all know that we all have our roles, and we all know that without one of us, it wouldn't work."

Harry on being in 1D.

CLEANLINESS CLAUSES

Being in a boyband isn't always as much fun as it looks! Harry's contract during the One Direction years reportedly included strict "cleanliness clauses" meaning he could be removed from the group if he failed to follow certain rules about behaviour and public image. Years later, when he signed his first solo contract without those restrictions, Harry admitted he "burst into tears" because he finally felt "truly free" as an artist.

One – and Done!

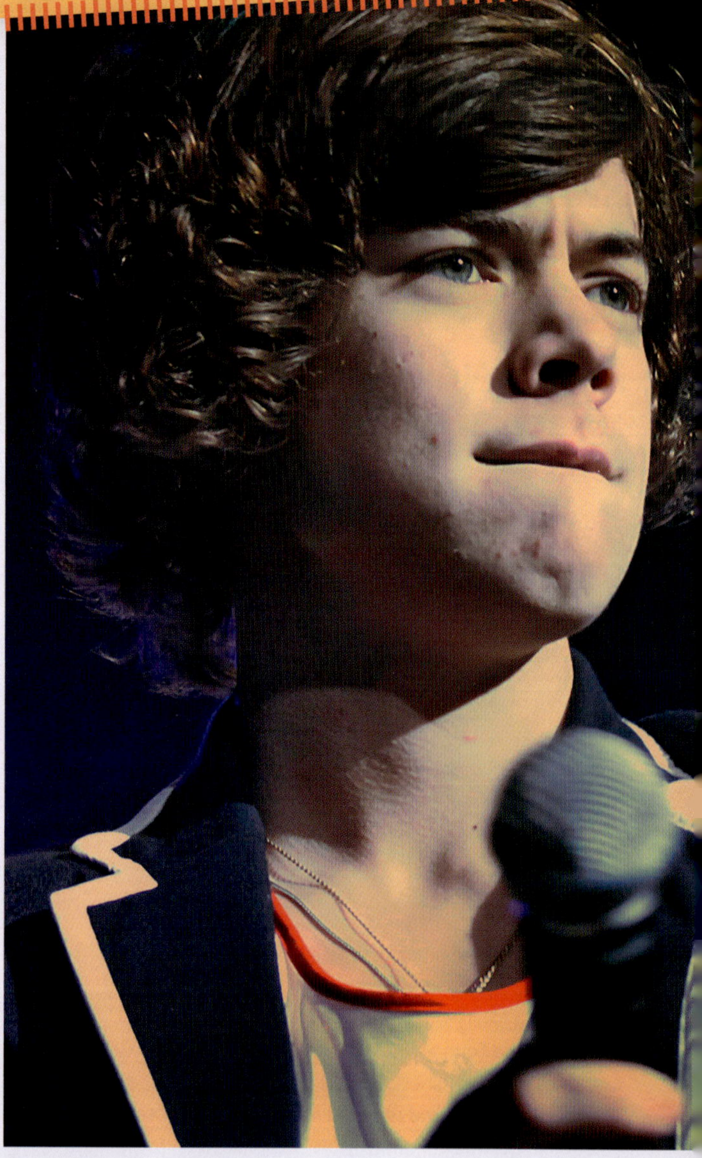

Where to start? With Harry as the group's unofficial leader, One Direction became the biggest thing to happen to their fans, the Directioners! The group's cultural legacy lingers even today ...

BEST. BAND. EVER.

One Direction – or 1D, as they quickly became known – went on to conquer the world despite not winning *The X Factor*, not even finishing second, and being five strangers who had never sung together before. They hadn't met, hadn't planned to be in a group, and weren't even sure they liked each other at first. Yet somehow, the unlikely band became the biggest boy band of their generation, selling more than 70 million records worldwide and building a massive – and loyal – global fanbase!

WHAT MAKES THEM BEAUTIFUL

The band's debut single **'What Makes You Beautiful'** was released on 11 September, 2011. Written by Savan Kotecha, the song's famous chorus was inspired by a real moment with his wife. "She was like, 'Oh, I feel so ugly,' and I was like, 'No, you look beautiful. You don't know how beautiful you look.' And I thought, 'That's a good song!'" Kotecha later revealed he has kept the texts from Harry after he first heard the demo: "I think you got it. I think you got The One here." No. 1 indeed: it became the band's first music video to receive one billion views on YouTube and went to No. 1 all over the world.

One Direction on their first ever tour.

UP ALL NIGHT

The boys released their debut album, *Up All Night*, on 21 November, 2011 in the UK, where it shot straight to No. 1 and became the UK's fastest-selling debut album of all time. When it was released in the US on 20 March, 2012, it made history by debuting at No. 1 – the first time a British act's debut album had topped the chart since the Beatles in 1964. The album included three songs co-written by Harry: **'Taken'**, **'Everything About You'** and **'Same Mistakes'**. Despite his position as unofficial leader of the group, he sings solo for only about seven minutes across the entire record's 45-minute duration.

ESSENTIAL PLAYLIST

One Direction released 109 songs. Are these their best?

1. Night Changes
2. What Makes You Beautiful
3. Story of My Life
4. Steal My Girl
5. Perfect **6.** You & I
7. 18 **8.** Drag Me Down
9. Best Song Ever
10. Right Now

> "I was 16 when One Direction started. I just finished school and didn't really know what it was that was happening. Everything was new and exciting, and I didn't know how long everything was going to last."

Harry on 1D's first fame.

GLOBAL ICONS

In just five years, One Direction shattered record after record, earning six Guinness World Records at the height of their fame and being named Billboard's Artist of the Year in 2014. Even years after their hiatus, their songs have been streamed more than 30 billion times on Spotify, with more than 40 million monthly listeners – and they've been inactive for ten years! Their biggest hit, **'Night Changes'**, has over 2.5 billion streams, and their YouTube videos have more than 14.5 billion views.

HARRYMANIA

With 1D's explosive worldwide fame, 'HarryMania' quickly singled him out as the band's brightest star. Whether it was his swoon-worthy curls, charm, flamboyant style or cheeky personality, he drew huge fan attention everywhere he went. "You're never going to get used to walking into a room and having people screaming at you," he admitted. Despite the chaos, Harry stayed grounded, crediting his friends and family for keeping him level-headed – and, unlike many stars his age, he has avoided major public scandals or meltdowns.

THE END OF AN ERA

"Please don't forget us – we will always be here for you. You guys are the most incredible fans," Harry said as One Direction walked off stage after their final performance, fittingly on *The X Factor* in December 2015. The band never performed together again. In 2024, Harry's beloved One Direction bandmate, Liam Payne, passed away and the world mourned when the news broke. At the funeral, all of Harry's bandmates reunited privately in grief – the first time they had been pictured together in ten years. A heartbreaking end to 1D's incredible era.

FOUR FROM FIVE

From 2011 to 2015, One Direction released five studio albums, each one boosting their fame and fanbase even further. After *Up All Night* (2011) came *Take Me Home* (2012), *Midnight Memories* (2013), *Four* (2014) and *Made in the A.M.* (2015) – all of which debuted at No. 1 in the UK. Their third album, *Midnight Memories*, became the world's biggest-selling album and after the release of *Four*, 1D became the first ever band in the history of the US Billboard charts to have their first four albums debut at No. 1 – proof, were it needed, that One Direction had truly taken over the planet!

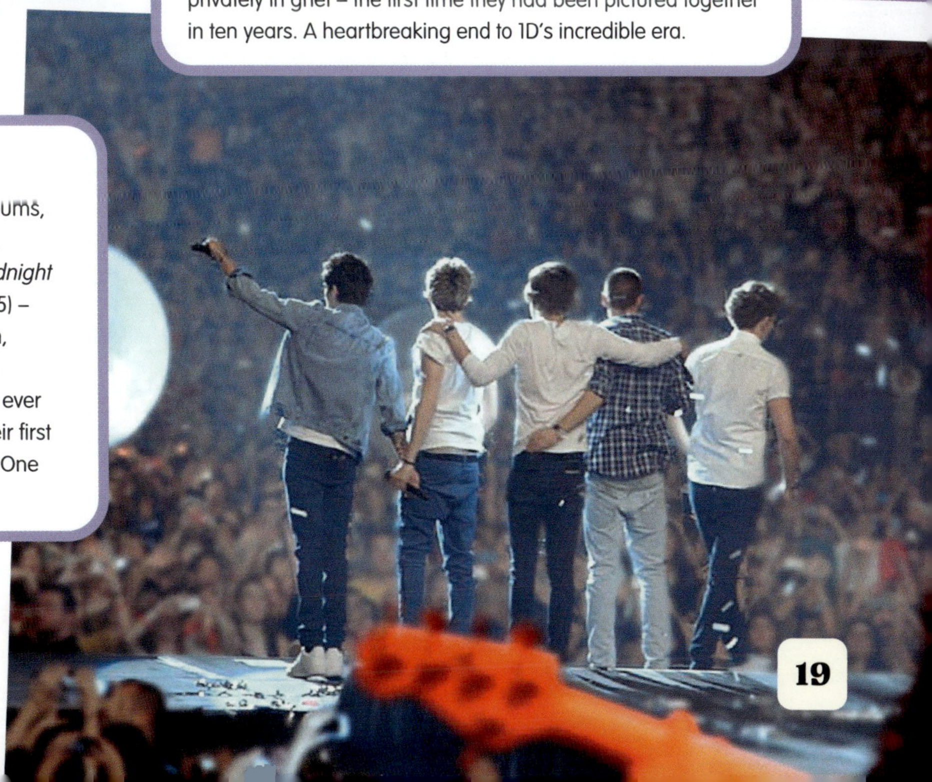

Best. Song. Ever.

Harry is now an award-winning songwriter in his own right, but a few songs stand out to him as personal favourites – whether they are his own solo tracks, songs he wrote for 1D, tracks created for other artists, or songs by the idols who inspired him growing up.

HIS FAVE 1D TRACK

Over the years, Harry has been asked many times about his favourite One Direction song. While there have been several answers, Harry most recently picked **'Heart Attack'** from the band's 2012 album *Take Me Home*. It was never released as a single, but he still loves it, saying he sometimes forgets about it until he hears it again and realises just how good it is. He also named another favourite: **'Happily'** from the 2013 album *Midnight Memories*. Go listen to both songs now!

HARRY'S BIGGEST 1D SONG

Possibly the biggest hit Harry co-wrote for One Direction was **'Story of My Life'**, released in 2013. It reached No. 2 on the UK Singles Chart and No. 6 on the US Billboard Hot 100. Harry has said he loves the song because it was one of the first to show a more emotional, grown-up side of the band. Fans loved the music video too, featuring childhood photos – including clips of Harry at age four. It reached one billion views in April 2025!

HARRY'S ULTIMATE MIXTAPE*

1. Girl from the North Country - Bob Dylan & Johnny Cash
2. The Chain - Fleetwood Mac
3. Ultralight Beam - Kanye West
4. A Change Is Gonna Come - Sam Cooke
5. Time - Pink Floyd
6. Wild Horses - The Rolling Stones
7. Heart of Gold - Neil Young
8. You've Got the Love - Candi Staton
9. Girl - The Beatles
10. Suspicious Minds - Elvis Presley

*Songs we know Harry loves!

HIS FAVOURITE SOLO SONG?

A favourite song from Harry's solo career is the album's title track and final song, **'Fine Line'**. Like **'Cherry'**, he didn't write it with the intention of releasing it as a single, which may be exactly why it means so much to him. The song feels deeply personal and emotional. Harry said, "Now when I listen to it, it's one of those things where I'm just proud that it's mine, I'm so happy. It's one of those songs that I've always wanted to make," showing how special the track is to him.

THE SONG HARRY WISHES HE'D WRITTEN

"I wish I had written **'50 Ways to Leave Your Lover'**. It's incredible!" Harry said of Paul Simon's classic 1975 track in 2019 when asked which song in pop history he wished he had written. He explained that he loves its verse melody, calling it "the greatest verse melody ever written." Do you agree?

100% UNOFFICIAL

TAYLOR'S SONG?

"If you're looking for someone to write your breakup songs about, baby, I'm perfect!" So, croons and swoons Harry on 1D's 2015 hit **'Perfect'**, which he co-wrote. Many fans believe the song playfully responds to Taylor Swift, who briefly dated Harry in 2012 and later released break-up songs thought to be about him, particularly one – **'Style'**. Its famous lyric describes "long hair, slicked back, white T-shirt", which listeners linked to Harry's look at the time. While neither star has confirmed the connection, Harry hasn't denied it either!

When Coldplay's Chris Martin performed the Harry-written track, **'Just A Little Bit Of Your Heart'**, with Ariana Grande at the Global Citizens festival in 2015, Chris introduced the song, saying: "This was written by the most handsome man in the world!", agreed.

Ariana singing 'Just A Little Bit Of Your Heart' at the Grammys.

SONGS FOR OTHER ARTISTS

Harry Styles has co-written several songs for other artists. He co-wrote **'Just a Little Bit of Your Heart'** with Johan Carlsson for Ariana Grande's second studio album *My Everything* (2014). Grande later performed the song at the 57th Annual Grammy Awards as a first-time nominee. "I was like crying when I heard the song he wrote for me," she said. "It's a beautiful song. He's an amazing writer." Harry also co-wrote **'Someday'** with Meghan Trainor, for Michael Bublé's Grammy-nominated ninth studio album *Nobody but Me* (2016).

"When I started songwriting, I really didn't know what I was doing. I tried to write as much as possible, with as many different people as possible and try and learn as much as I could. I guarantee I wrote a lot of really, really bad stuff before I wrote anything good."

Harry on the evolution of his songwriting.

Harry Styles

On 12 May, 2017, two years after One Direction's hiatus, Harry stepped out as a solo star and proved he was far more than a boyband heartthrob. He was an artist in his own right. Naturally, his solo debut went to No. 1 everywhere ...

Harry flies high in his 'Sign of the Times' video.

SIGNED, SEALED, DELIVERED!

In May 2016, Harry signed a recording contract with Columbia Records, a squiggly signature that marked the official start of his solo career. Harry describes the moment as one where he felt "truly free" as an artist. He was in good company too. Columbia Records is home to the world's biggest artists, and Harry's heroes: Beyoncé, Adele, Bob Dylan, Bruce Springsteen, Barbra Streisand, Celine Dion, Daft Punk, Pharrell Williams and Lil Nas X.

HIS MOST INTIMATE MOMENT – SO FAR

Harry has said repeatedly over the years that his debut solo album was the most personal piece of work he had ever completed, hence why Harry wanted to title it, simply: *Harry Styles*. The ten songs defined who he was, and who he wasn't, following the breakdown of his former band. "I wanted to put out a piece of me that I haven't put out before," Harry said. "I didn't want to write 'stories'. I wanted to write my stories, things that happened to me. The number one thing was I wanted to be honest. I hadn't done that before."

TICKLED PINK

During its production, Harry's debut album was originally called Pink. He chose the name because, as he explained, "Pink is the true colour of rock and roll," showing how strongly the record was inspired by classic rock rather than modern pop. Although the title was later changed, the idea lived on in the artwork. The album's cover and sleeve feature a soft shade known as 'millennial pink', because of its popularity among that demographic.

SEVENTY SONGS LONG

Recorded in Jamaica over a 12-month period in 2016, Harry's debut album almost looked very different – at one point, he had more than 70 songs to choose from. Songs his fans may never hear! Harry travelled to Jamaica with his regular collaborators – Jeff Bhasker, Kid Harpoon, Tyler Johnson, Alex Salibian and Mitch Rowland – to write and record, staying in a remote studio space where they could focus without any distractions. Being far away from 'everyday life' helped Harry experiment with new sounds and figure out his own style after One Direction.

FIRST TIME AS SONGWRITER

For the first time in his career, Harry was the frontman of his own music, a challenge he truly enjoyed. Instead of using lots of outside songwriters, he worked with a small, trusted group and focused on songs that felt personal, often starting alone at the piano. Writing became a safe way for him to express his feelings. "I found it really therapeutic to write," he said, explaining that being at an instrument helped him open up in a way talking sometimes couldn't. "It was tough to really delve in and find out who you are as a writer but also … heaven."

SIGN OF THE TIMES

While Harry Styles introduce three big solo singles, including **'Kiwi'** and **'Two Ghosts'**, it was Harry's lead single that sent the solo singer stratospheric – again! **'Sign of the Times'** reached No. 1 on the UK Singles Chart, No.4 on the Billboard Hot 100 and topped the charts in more than 80 countries! It remains one of Harry's favourite, and most important, tracks: it was the song deliberately chosen to introduce him as a serious male artist. It's also a song with a crucial message. "We happen to be in a time where things happening around the world are absolutely impossible to ignore – just the state of the world at the moment," Harry has said. "I think it would've been strange to not acknowledge what was going on at all. **'Sign of the Times'**, for example, is me commenting on how difficult things are."

Harry performs for the *Today* show, 2017.

"I really wanted to make an album that I wanted to listen to. That was the only way I knew I wouldn't look back on it and regret it. It was more, 'What do I want to sit and listen to?' rather than, 'How do I shake up compared to what's on radio right now?'"

Harry on his debut solo album.

TRACK LIST

1. Meet Me In The Hallway
2. Sign of the Times
3. Carolina 4. Two Ghosts
5. Sweet Creature
6. Only Angel 7. Kiwi
8. Ever Since New York
9. Woman
10. From The Dining Table

What's your favourite track?

Live On Tour!

Harry's very first solo world tour began on 19 September, 2017 in San Francisco and included 89 shows across 25 countries. About one million tickets were released – and they sold out in just 29 seconds! Were you lucky enough to be there?

SET LIST

***Live On Tour* 2017–18**

Only Angel, Woman, Ever Since New York, Two Ghosts, Carolina, Stockholm Syndrome, Just a Little Bit of Your Heart, Medicine, Meet Me in the Hallway, Sweet Creature, If I Could Fly, Anna, What Makes You Beautiful, Sign of the Times, Encore, From the Dining Table, The Chain, Kiwi.

UP CLOSE AND PERSONAL

The *Live On Tour* shows may not have been as big (or as loud!) as those Harry experienced as a member of One Direction, but they were designed to better suit him as a solo artist who wanted a more intimate experience with his fans. It was Harry's decision to play smaller venues for the first leg of the tour, giving fans the chance to feel closer to him. The tour began in theatres in 2017 before moving to larger arenas in 2018. "The crowd is so emotionally generous that they just want me to be having a good time, and I want to feel that," Harry said.

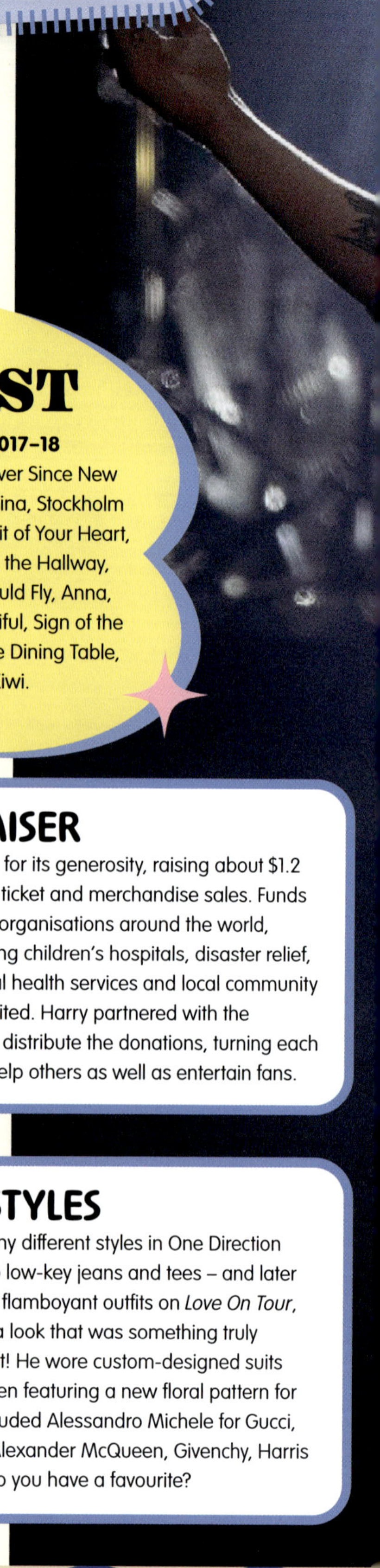

Harry at Los Angeles's Hollywood Bowl.

FUN FUNDRAISER

The tour was also praised for its generosity, raising about $1.2 million for charity through ticket and merchandise sales. Funds were shared between 62 organisations around the world, including groups supporting children's hospitals, disaster relief, LGBTQIA+ charities, mental health services and local community projects in the cities he visited. Harry partnered with the nonprofit Global Citizen to distribute the donations, turning each concert into a chance to help others as well as entertain fans.

NEXT LEVEL STYLES

Harry may have worn many different styles in One Direction – from preppy sweaters to low-key jeans and tees – and later dazzled fans with sparkly, flamboyant outfits on *Love On Tour*, but for this tour he chose a look that was something truly different – and magnificent! He wore custom-designed suits by top fashion houses, often featuring a new floral pattern for each show. Designers included Alessandro Michele for Gucci, Calvin Klein, Raf Simons, Alexander McQueen, Givenchy, Harris Reed and Saint Laurent. Do you have a favourite?

Harry takes a bow in Gucci for the US leg of Live on Tour.

HARRY'S THOUGHTS ABOUT THE TOUR

"This tour affected me deeply. It really changed me emotionally. Having people come to sing my songs. The fans in the room make this environment where people come to feel like they can be themselves. There's nothing that makes me feel more myself than to be in this whole room of people. It made me realise people want to see me experiment and have fun."

HARRY MAKES A CALL

"Good evening, Los Angeles, my name is Harry, it's such a pleasure to see you all tonight. I have one job tonight and that's to entertain you. I'll do my very best!" With those words, Harry opened the final night of *Live On Tour* at Los Angeles' legendary Forum. And, moments later, he proved it when a fan threw her phone on stage, hoping for a photo. Instead, Harry noticed it was unlocked and cheekily called the fan's mother to chat about her daughter and the concert. "Hello. Consider this a voicemail," he said. "I hope you are enjoying the show. Your daughter threw her phone on stage. Do with her what you will." Iconic!

Fine Line

A Christmas present for his fans, Harry's second album was released on 13 December, 2019. It more than doubled the sales of his first album and was described on numerous occasions as a "gorgeous dollop of Los Angeles-tinged pop".

Harry gets fruity in the Watermelon Sugar video.

TREAT PEOPLE WITH KINDNESS, PT.1

A fan favourite and an anthemic live highlight from *Fine Line*, **'Treat People With Kindness'** quickly became a concert classic, boosted by its joyful video starring Phoebe Waller-Bridge. The title turned into the guiding motto of *Love On Tour* and a message Harry wanted every show to share. "I wanted the song to be a mantra for the tour," he said. "It's universal and important, a small change that makes a big difference" for everyone. On tour, during the song, fans often started a long conga line!

GONNA BE GOLDEN

'Golden' was the very first song written for *Fine Line* – and the fourth single – and created on the second day of sessions at Shangri-La Studios in Malibu, California. It went on to become one of the album's brightest and most popular tracks. A breezy slice of California pop, it was also Harry's favourite recording memory, started from some chords he had on the guitar. "When we wrote **'Golden'**, we were sitting around the kitchen … there were five of us singing harmonies," he recalled. It was always the first song he played people when they came to the studio and was destined to open the album.

Harry's jumpsuit just popped a button – again!

WATERMELON SUGAR – HI!

Watermelons are 91 per cent water, making them super hydrating, and they are packed with vitamins A and C plus potassium and magnesium. But enough about Harry's favourite snack. His 2019 hit **'Watermelon Sugar'** was partly inspired by the 1968 novel *In Watermelon Sugar* by Richard Brautigan, a copy of which was in the studio. The book is about a dreamlike community where people live simple lives in a strange world made of watermelon sugar!

ADORE YOU

The second single from *Fine Line*, **'Adore You'**, is one of the album's poppiest tracks, something Harry highlighted during promotion. It marked his return to bright, fun pop after the more serious tone of his debut album, *Harry Styles*. The song grew out of late-night chats with guitarist Mitch Rowland about legends like David Bowie, Paul Simon and Van Morrison balancing serious songs with playful ones. It later won Most Performed Work at the 2021 Ivor Novello Awards, largely in part for its two billion streams – and counting!

HARRY'S MOST FUN ALBUM?

If Harry's debut solo album was about introducing him as a serious artist, *Fine Line* was about having fun and letting his hair down. During the two years making the record, he went through major personal changes (he famously started therapy) and said he finally felt comfortable being himself. "With *Fine Line* I let go of the fear of getting it wrong and … it was really joyous and really free. I think with music it's so important to evolve – and that extends to clothes and videos. That's why you look back at David Bowie with Ziggy Stardust or the Beatles and their different eras – that fearlessness is super inspiring."

SIX HIT SINGLES

You know an album is a blockbuster when it spins off six hit singles: **'Lights Up'**, **'Adore You'**, **'Falling'**, **'Watermelon Sugar'**, **'Golden'** and **'Treat People With Kindness'**. Few albums manage that many releases from one era. Shania Twain's *Come On Over* (1997) and Michael Jackson's *Thriller* both yielded multiple hit singles – and they are two of the top 10 bestselling albums of all time!

A FINE SUCCESS

Fine Line was Harry's first mega-million selling solo success. It debuted at No. 1 on the Billboard 200 in the US with the biggest opening sales for a UK male artist there at the time, giving him his second consecutive No. 1 album. It was nominated for Album of the Year at the 2020 BRIT Awards and Best Pop Vocal Album at the 2021 Grammys. **'Watermelon Sugar'** won Best Pop Solo Performance, and Rolling Stone later ranked the album at No. 491 on its 500 Greatest Albums of All Time list.

100% UNOFFICIAL

> Making *Fine Line*, the times where I was really happy were the happiest of my life, but the times where I was a little lower were the saddest times.

Harry on Fine Line.

TRACK LIST

1. Golden
2. Watermelon Sugar
3. Adore You **4.** Lights Up
5. Cherry **6.** Falling
7. To Be So Lonely **8.** She
9. Sunflower, Vol. 6
10. Canyon Moon
11. Treat People with Kindness
12. Fine Line

What's your favourite track?

Best. Show. Ever.

With more than 800 shows under his belt before turning 30, Harry has become one of the most prolific and passionate performers of his generation ... as these shows, well, show!

Will the luscious long locks ever return?

HARRY'S FIRST GIG

OK, so not a show of his own, but still an important moment in Harry's musical upbringing. On 2 February, 2008, Harry's sister Gemma bought tickets for Harry's birthday to see The Rocket Summer at Manchester Club Academy, not far from where he lived with his mum and sister. The Rocket Summer is the solo project of singer-songwriter Bryce Avary, blending pop-punk, piano-rock and heartfelt lyrics with energetic, joyful performances. Sound familiar? "It was good," Harry later said.

1D IN 3D

The first time Harry ever performed in three-dimensions as one-fifth of One Direction was at the opening night of their first ever headline show, in support of their debut album *Up All Night* at The Colosseum, Watford, on 18 December, 2011. All the boys were beyond nervous as they performed 13 original songs, and a handful of covers, including The Black Eyed Peas' **'I Gotta Feeling'**, The Zutons' **'Valerie'** and **'Use Somebody'** by Kings of Leon. Were you there?

The 1D brothers in their preppy era!

COACHELLA 2022

This famous gig has become iconic to Harry's fans as the first ever live outing of the global smash hit **'As It Was'** – the concert's opening tune. Imagine being there for that! For this now-legendary show, in front of 100,000 fans, Harry wore a custom-sequinned jumpsuit designed by Gucci. Harry is the only former One Direction member to headline the iconic music festival in southern California. It was a huge personal milestone, and Harry later called the moment "a dream come true".

FEATHER BOA TIME

If you want to know where Harry's fans get their love of feather boas, look no further than his now-legendary **'Watermelon Sugar'** performance at the 2021 Grammy Awards in Los Angeles. Just before winning Best Pop Solo Performance for the song, Harry delivered a sun-soaked version with a full horn section, wearing a black leather suit and a bright green feather boa. Everything about it was iconic! And it was just one of three different feather boas he wore that night.

WEMBLEY REVELATIONS

Proof that dreams really do come true, Harry played his first four-night sold-out run at London's legendary Wembley Stadium in June 2023, among the final shows of *Love On Tour*. During one concert, he spotted a pregnant fan holding a sign asking for a gender reveal. "Are you sure you want to do this with all those people?" he joked before counting down with the crowd. As pink confetti exploded into the air, Harry announced, "We're having a girl, Wembley!" and the stadium went wild.

TINY DESK

Some of the most-watched video content on YouTube is NPR's *Tiny Desk* concerts, where the world's most famous artists perform intimate, stripped-back sets from behind, well, a tiny desk! These mini-gigs are designed to showcase a singer's vocal ability and musicianship. On 25 February, 2020, Harry performed an unforgettable four-song set: **'Cherry'**, **'Watermelon Sugar'**, **'To Be So Lonely'** and **'Adore You'**. It has over 34 million views – one of NPR's most watched sets!

"I get a front-row seat to see a bunch of people getting in a room together and just being themselves, dancing like nobody's watching. A room full of people just loving each other is so powerful."

Harry on performing live for his fans.

Harry making his superhero debut as Eros.

Harry as his *Dunkirk* character, Alex.

Harry Goes to Hollywood

Harry's love of the movies goes far beyond his song 'Cinema'. He's also made the leap to the silver screen, starring in several major Hollywood films.

BROTHER OF THANOS

He may only be on screen for no more than 30 seconds, but Harry's mid-credits scene in Marvel's *Eternals* (2021) was deliberately designed as a tease rather than a full performance, setting up a potential future Marvel storyline. Harry was cast by the film's director, Chloé Zhao, as Eros, a cosmic adventurer and the brother of the supervillain Thanos, the main bad guy from Marvel's blockbuster *Infinity Saga*.

SOLDIER ON, HARRY!

Harry made his film debut as Alex, a young British soldier in Christopher Nolan's World War II 2017 drama, *Dunkirk*. He cut his long, luscious popstar hair for the role and was praised for delivering a restrained, natural performance. The director signed Harry up for the role without even realising who he was! "I don't think I was that aware really of how famous Harry was," Nolan has said. "My daughter had talked about him. I cast Harry because he fit the part wonderfully and truly earned a seat at the table. Harry was perfect for this part." When asked about cutting his hair, Harry said, "I don't want to get into it!"

> What I like about acting is I feel like I have no idea what I'm doing. Making music is a really personal thing. There are aspects of acting where you're drawing from experiences a bit, but for the most part you're pretending to play someone else. That's what I find the most interesting about it.

Harry on pretending to be someone else!

NEARLY ELVIS

In 2022, acclaimed director Baz Luhrmann released his biopic of American icon Elvis Presley, titled *Elvis*. The title role ultimately went to Austin Butler, but the part nearly went to another well-known heartthrob – Harry. Why didn't he get it? Because the director felt Harry was too famous to play Elvis.

HARRY'S FAVOURITE MOVIES

Harry has revealed on many occasions his favourite obsessions, from music to movies, inspirations to influences. He's mad about *Love Actually*, *Titanic* and *Bohemian Rhapsody*, but his favourite film of all time – and one he repeatedly "circles back to" – is Nicholas Sparks' *The Notebook*. The film stars Ryan Gosling and Rachel McAdams as young lovers from different worlds who fall deeply in love one summer, before being torn apart by circumstance. It's a tearjerker for sure!

THIS IS US

Long before Hollywood called, Harry was smashing it on the silver screen in *One Direction: This Is Us*, a documentary charting their rise to global superstardom, blending concert performances with behind-the-scenes footage. The film was a hit, zooming to No. 1 in multiple countries. Of the film crew following him around all day Harry said, "It was kind of just getting on with the day as normal, but there was someone in your way when you tried to get out of a door." Classic.

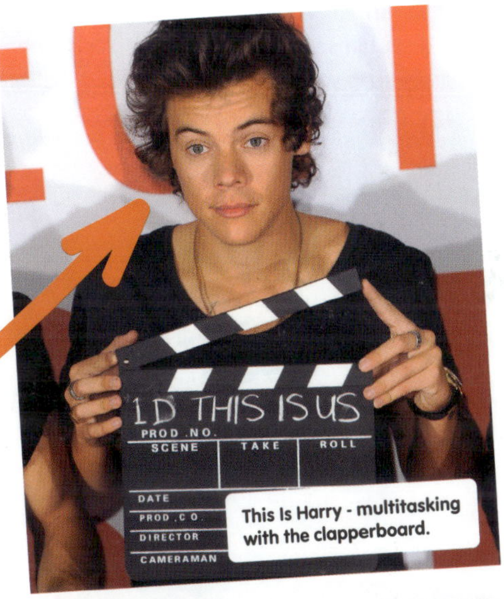

This Is Harry - multitasking with the clapperboard.

HIT THE ROAD, JACK

In 2022, Harry signed on to play the role of Jack Chambers, a seemingly devoted husband to Florence Pugh in Olivia Wilde's psychological drama, *Don't Worry, Darling*. The role was Harry's first leading part in a major Hollywood movie and won him praise from many of his peers, he was even called a "revelation" by the director, Wilde. Fun fact: Harry and Olivia dated for more than two years after the movie was released.

Harry and Florence Pugh in *Don't Worry, Darling*.

What Makes YOU Beautiful

Harry loves his fans – that means YOU! – more than anything else in the world. He has the most loyal and loving fanbase, and enjoys nothing more than getting up close and personal with them!

WHAT ARE YOU?

Are you with the Harries or the Stylers? Both names are widely used to describe Harry's fanbase, and there is no official winner, with fans happily choosing whichever they prefer. 'Harries' feels cute and classic, while 'Stylers' sounds a bit more fashion forward and cool. Harry himself has never officially picked one, so the choice is totally up to you. Personally, we think Stylers is, well … more stylish! Which nickname would *you* pick?

SWEET CREATURES

The Harry Styles Rainbow Project was a fan-led surprise during *Love On Tour*, most famously at London's O2 Arena in April 2018. Fans held coloured paper over their phone lights to turn the entire crowd into a giant rainbow flag, usually during **'Sweet Creature'**. The plan, organised on social media, aimed to create a safe and welcoming space to celebrate pride and inclusivity. Thousands joined in to produce a powerful moment of unity that Harry himself had not planned. Its creators, Ksenia and Luna, dreamt up the idea and within 24 hours of setting up a dedicated Twitter account, their first post received more than 1,000 retweets and other fans began to offer help.

MEET HARRY, THE FISH

Perhaps the cutest, coolest moment ever: in October 2019 in Hampstead, North London, Harry's car broke down on a residential street outside of the home of superfan Theadora. She, unbelievably, wasn't in. Argh! But he did leave a handwritten note apologising for missing her. "Theadora, your dad's friend kindly let me wait at your house with a cup of tea. I'm devastated that we missed each other. Looking forward to meeting soon. Treat people with kindness." He also noted that he fed her fish, took photos with said fish and signed her copy of his album *Fine Line*. Theadora later revealed the name of her fish. Yes, you've guessed it: Harry.

PIZZA AND KIWIS

A group of loyal fans faced a long, cold night when they camped out overnight on the streets of New York City. They were queuing up for tickets to see Harry perform on the comedy TV show, *Saturday Night Live*, on 14 April, 2017, ahead of his debut solo appearance. Harry, being Harry, surprised them with hot pizzas, coffees and, most unexpectedly, a platter of kiwis! Fans thought it hinted at a song choice, but it did not. One fan wrote online, "We asked Harry why he gave us kiwi and he just shrugged and smiled." Classic Harry.

> While I was in 1D, I was constantly scared of getting things wrong. Now, as a solo artist, I feel like the fans have given me an environment to be myself and grow up and create this safe space to learn and make mistakes.

Harry talks about his fan base.

Over the years, Harry's fans have raised huge amounts of money for charitable causes in support of the charities he cares about.

HARRY DEFENDS HIS YOUNG FANS

Starting in his One Direction days, Harry has always defended the millions of young, mainly female, fans who support him. Critics often claimed they were not there for the music, just to watch him, but Harry strongly disagreed. "We're so past that dumb outdated narrative of 'Oh, these people are girls, so they don't know what they're talking about.' They're the ones who know what they're talking about! They're the people who listen obsessively. They own it. They're running it." For Harry, their passion has always deserved respect, not dismissal.

Mister Fashionista

Styles could not be a more perfect surname for a man with such an awesome eye for fashion, styling and being ahead of the trend at all times. Lets enjoy some of Harry's most notable outfits ...

Was this the beginning of his jumpsuit obsession? We think so!

THE START OF HIS STYLE

Harry has always had a flair for standing out, especially when it comes to costumes. In One Direction he often grabbed attention, and it was the same at school. During his primary years at Hermitage Primary School in Holmes Chapel, Cheshire, he was cast as Barney, a church mouse, in a school play. Harry later laughed about how "crazy" it felt to perform wearing tights. "But, that was maybe where it all kicked off!" he joked, hinting at his future love of fancy dress.

TEENAGE KICKS

When he was in One Direction, Harry was the first member to embrace a more fashion-forward look. In 2013, when he was named Britain's Most Stylish person, he was known for skinny jeans, Chelsea boots and band T-shirts. He later recalled getting strange looks when he wore the outfit back home in Holmes Chapel. "People were like, 'What are you wearing? They're not football trainers.'"

THE 2019 MET GALA

Harry's first truly striking outfit that blurred the lines between menswear and womenswear came when he co-hosted the 2019 Met Gala in New York. He wore a custom black Gucci ensemble designed by Alessandro Michele and pierced his ear to add a pearl earring for the occasion. The look featured a sheer black lace blouse with a bow and high-waisted trousers. "I think what's exciting about right now is you can wear what you like. It doesn't have to be X or Y," Harry has said.

The Boy with the Pearl Earring.

No clowning around. This outfit is peak Harry.

Following the release of the 'As It Was' music video, searches for jumpsuits increased by a massive 212 per cent during its release week!

CRYSTAL JUMPSUIT

Over the years Harry has worn countless glittery jumpsuits which, along with floral suits, feather boas, oversized brooches and pearls, have become his signature evening wear. At the 2023 Grammy Awards, he arrived in The One Jumpsuit To Rule Them All: a custom low cut, multicoloured harlequin jumpsuit by EgonLab – covered in 250,000 Swarovski rhinestones of rainbow colours! It was dazzling and impossible to miss. It was also just one of three outfit changes that night. (To be fair, he did go home with a Grammy.)

A STYLISH SORE THUMB

It was at the 2015 American Music Awards, one of Harry's final major appearances with One Direction, that fans first noticed him setting himself apart stylistically. He wore a bold floral Gucci suit, a look he returned to during his first solo tour the following year. Compared with his bandmates, Harry's fashion choices really stood out, but they had a purpose: they boosted his confidence. "I'll put on something that feels really flamboyant, and I don't feel crazy wearing it," he has said. "I think if you get something that you feel amazing in, it's like a superhero outfit."

HARRY MAKES HISTORY

In December 2020, Harry made history as the first man to appear solo on the cover of American Vogue. It sold an additional 40,000 subscriptions after the cover was launched and a second print run with a waitlist had to be ordered! The magazine, founded in 1892, has had more than 3,000 cover stars! Photographed by fashion icon Tyler Mitchell, Harry challenged traditional gender norms by wearing a lace-trimmed Gucci ballgown with a tuxedo jacket. In the magazine, Harry said: "There's so much joy to be had in playing with clothes."

OFF-DUTY HARRY

When Harry isn't on-stage, on a red carpet, or on a chat show, he can be seen in much more relaxed attire. Fans call this his 'off-duty' look. In April 2025, he was pictured in a simple cotton-canvas jacket with wide-legged Valentino trousers and a pair of loafers – stylish, but simple.

Harry in green should always be seen!

Florals for spring? Not Harry. He wears them in November for the AMAs.

Music For A Video Star

Harry has blessed us with scores of weird and wonderful music videos over the years, proving that he is not just a star of the big screen, but a creative genius on the small screen too.

VIDEO OF THE YEAR

Harry's become accustomed to winning awards for his looks and his music, but in 2018, Harry won his first BRIT award as a solo performer (1D won a total of seven awards!). Harry won British Video of the Year for his debut single, **'Sign of the Times'**. Unfortunately, Harry was absent on the night to collect his trophy, so host Jack Whitehall gave it away to singer Olly Murs instead, joking that Olly had never won a BRIT before.

THIS IS US

Harry's first foray into film was released in 2013 with *One Direction: This Is Us*. A genuine box office blockbuster, the movie gave fans an inside look at the band's meteoric rise. Directed by Morgan Spurlock, the film mixed behind the scenes tour footage with personal stories from Harry, Niall, Liam, Louis and Zayn. It debuted at No. 1 in several countries and earned more than $68 million worldwide. For many fans, it was the first time seeing the boys beyond the boyband, and as real people with relatable personalities. It also introduced audiences to Harry's loveable, former bakery colleagues!

STARRING PHOEBE WALLER-BRIDGE

After watching *Fleabag* writer and star Phoebe Waller-Bridge perform her show on-stage in London, Harry invited her to appear in the **'Treat People With Kindness'** video, released on 1 January, 2021. The clip was inspired by the 1943 film *Stormy Weather*, featuring the Nicholas Brothers' famous dance routine. Director Gabe Turner wanted Harry and Phoebe to recreate that joyful style with help from choreographer Paul Roberts. Dressed in matching Gucci outfits, the pair showed great chemistry as Harry sings, "I just keep on dancing."

YOU GOT ME THINKING OF DAYLIGHT

"If I was a bluebird, I would fly to you," sings Harry in **'Daylight'**, the fifth single from *Harry's House*, a song about longing and long-distance love. In the official video, he wears a yellow, feathered jumpsuit and tries to fly to his lover, with chaotic results! There is also a second version directed by his friend James Corden, filmed for just $300 in about three hours for *The Late Late Show*. It is scrappy, funny and surprisingly charming. Check it out!

> In music, there's such an immediate response to what you do. You finish a song and people clap. When you're filming a movie and they say 'Cut,' you expect everyone to start clapping, but they don't. Everyone just goes back to doing their jobs, and you're like, 'Oh, no, was it that bad?'

Harry on acting.

LATE NIGHT TALKING

One of Harry's most inventive – and revealing – music videos is for **'Late Night Talking'**, directed by acclaimed director duo Bradley & Pablo and released on 13 July, 2022. It shows Harry travelling through a series of surreal beds in different locations, from an art gallery to the streets of London. Fun details include a cameo from his real-life goddaughter, Ruby Winston, and scenes inspired by his dreams and sleepwalking. It was nominated for Song of Summer at the 2022 MTV Video Music Awards but lost to Jack Harlow's video for **'First Class'**.

LET THE LIGHT IN

On 23 January, 2026, Harry released his first music video in more than three years with **'Aperture'**. The song broke the record for the biggest debut by a male solo artist in Spotify history, earning over 12.47 million streams on day one. The video echoes David Bowie's **'I'm Afraid of Americans'**, showing Harry pursued by a mysterious man in sunglasses. A tense standoff turns into a chase, a tumble downstairs and a fight. It was filmed at Los Angeles's famous Westin Bonaventure Hotel, a location used in loads of films and other music videos.

HARRY WANTS TO KISS YOU

With more than half a billion views on YouTube, One Direction's **'Kiss You'** is perhaps the band's silliest video and one that brilliantly shows off Harry's cheeky sense of humour with the band making funny faces throughout. In the video, the band recreate a number of classic boyband tropes and clearly have a lot of fun in the process. Eagle-eyed viewers will notice that when Harry is "surfing" he covers his top two nipples – and then his two other nipples; he's got four remember – by far the video's funniest moment. It's at the 2 minutes and 55 seconds mark, in case you want to skip to it.

Harry Treats People Kindly

Harry believes in equal rights for everyone. His life's mission, and mantra, is to treat everyone he meets with kindness, and to turn his concerts into the ultimate safe space for all people ...

HARRY CUTS HIS HAIR

In May 2016, Harry broke the Internet – again! – and many of his fans' hearts when he cut off his long flowing locks for the film *Dunkirk*. Harry had been growing his hair for most of the time he was in 1D. "I want to shave my hair off, and no one will really let me," he said during the time. "Everyone's telling me not to do it. And my argument is, like, I think my popularity is in my face, and not my hair." When the time came to cut his hair off, he did so for the Little Princess Trust charity, which provides real hair wigs for children who suffer hair loss. Harry revealed the cut to the world on his Insta, showing him holding his cut off ponytail while giving a thumbs up along the words: "Whoops".

Which lovely locks look do you prefer?

LGBTQIA+ ICON

A fierce champion of the LGBTQIA+ community from his earliest days, Harry has shown the power of his Pride multiple times, supporting LGBT rights, trans rights and gender equality charities. Harry has also helped several fans come out at his gigs. Famously, at a November 2021 *Love On Tour* stop in Milwaukee, Harry read out the sign of fan McKinley McConnell: "My mom Lisa is in Section 201. Help me come out!". Harry stopped the show and shouted, "Lisa, she's gay!" to thunderous cheers from 17,000 fans. McKinley posted on X the next day and it went viral. "Thank you for creating a safe place for me."

HOORAY FOR HARRY!

In the last ten years, Harry has raised more than $6.5 million for charities such as Save the Children, CARE and the Rebuild Foundation, giving hope and help to countless people in need. Money from his tours, merchandise and special projects has gone towards helping children, families and communities in need around the world. Harry often encourages his fans to be kind and make a difference too, proving that even small actions can help change someone's life for the better.

TREAT PEOPLE WITH KINDNESS

'Treat People with Kindness' is the slogan Harry has used since 2017 to promote his message of love, acceptance and kindness to others. The slogan first came from a small badge pin Harry had on his guitar strap, which he then made into T-shirts that he sold on his website. When he started seeing a lot of the T-shirts at gigs and on the street, he realised it had connected with not just his fans, but everyone. "Oh, this is a bit of a thing!" he noted. The support for the slogan gave Styles the idea to write the iconic song with the same name.

Flying Start: Harry's first charitable cause.

> We're living in a time where it's impossible not to be aware of what's going on in the world. It's important to stand up for what we think is right. I would love for my views to come through in the music I make. That's a very powerful way that we can use our voices.

Harry on speaking up.

HELP FOR HEROES

Harry's journey of helping others began back in 2010 when he was one of the sixteen finalists on *The X Factor*. To raise money for Help for Heroes – a charity that supports wounded British servicemen and women – One Direction recorded a cover of David Bowie's iconic song **'Heroes'**, one of Harry's all-time favourites. The powerful charity single united the contestants for a meaningful cause and introduced the brand-new band to millions of viewers across the UK.

The last time Harry's been spotted in a tracksuit. Probably.

The Harry Phenomenon

Why has Harry become so successful? Is it his looks, his smile, his charm, his acting, his music, or a combination of them all? He has the X Factor, for sure – but what specifically is it that makes him so phenomenal?

> People ask for advice and I by no means feel like I'm in a place to give it because I feel like I still don't know anything.

Harry on advice to young musicians.

IN GOOD COMPANY

Harry Styles has sold over 30 million records worldwide as a solo artist and more than 70 million with One Direction, taking his overall total to more than 100 million albums. This places him among pop greats such as Paul McCartney, Michael Jackson and Phil Collins, rare artists who have each sold more than 100 million records both as solo stars and as members of hugely successful bands – and Harry is not even 35 yet!

HARRY'S AN ART-THROB

Like Bad Bunny and Billy Porter, Harry represents a new kind of male pop star – one who challenges ideas about how men 'should' look or act, and one who is just as happy wearing a beautiful dress as he is a sharp suit. He has helped popularise men wearing more daring and creative fashion, including pearl necklaces, Hawaiian shirts, Chelsea boots, wide-leg trousers and cosy knitwear. Put simply, Harry is an art-throb!

POPTIMISM

Harry may be a genre-blurring solo artist, mixing 70s rock influences with modern pop, but he is also part of a new wave of musical thinking: poptimism (a blend of pop and optimism). This movement believes pop music deserves the same critical respect, artistic merit and serious analysis as rock. For Harry, great pop is great art. The message and music Harry is spreading is rooted in joy and positivity.

ARISE, SIR HARRY!

A few years ago, Harry said he hoped to use his charity work and huge popularity to one day receive a knighthood. "I want to get my knighthood too one day." he said. He met the future King and Queen – Prince William and Catherine – at the Royal Variety Show in 2014 and was polite and respectful, so his chances of being knighted one day could be looking good! We think Sir Styles has a nice ring to it!

Britain's Most Wanted – hard at work.

ANTI-SOCIAL

Harry may be anti-social and no longer use social media directly – to protect his mental health – but that does not stop him from being one of the most followed entertainers on Earth. In 2026, his official Instagram account, @harrystyles, had more than 48 million followers and, let's face it, it will probably grow even more – maybe even double! – after Harry embarks on his *Together, Together* tour. Will you be one of the fans checking in for updates and behind the scenes sneak peeks?

UNDER THE INFLUENCE

Many musicians say they are inspired by Harry Styles and would love to work with him. Artists including SZA, Miley Cyrus, Elton John, Olivia Rodrigo, Chris Stapleton, Mark Ronson, Halsey, Lorde, Matty Healy, John Legend and Troye Sivan have praised his music and creativity. Others – including Jorja Smith, Arcade Fire, Kelly Clarkson, Kygo, Ellie Goulding, Sabrina Carpenter, Little Mix, Lizzo, Måneskin and Jungkook – have covered his songs. If you want to listen to emerging artists who cite Harry as a major influence, seek out: Joy Crookes, Mimi Webb, Ny Oh, Dayglow, Still Woozy, Muna and Moses Sumney. For those of you wondering why Harry rarely collaborates, it's because he calls himself a "very antisocial musician".

THE IDEA OF YOU

In 2024, Anne Hathaway starred as Solène Marchand in *The Idea of You*, a film based on the novel by Robinne Lee, which grew out of fan fiction she had been writing. The story follows a 40-year-old mother who falls in love with a much younger boyband star, Hayes Campbell, a character widely rumoured to be inspired by Harry and his relationship with director Olivia Wilde and reflecting his reputed past interest in older women. It's never been confirmed but the parallels are there! The film's composer was also Savan Kotecha, co-writer of One Direction's **'What Makes You Beautiful'**.

In 2023, it was announced that Texas State University would offer a course on our boy, titled "Harry Styles and the Cult of Celebrity: Identity, the Internet and European Pop Culture". The class examines how Harry's career connects to topics such as gender and sexuality, race, class, nation and globalism, media, fashion, fan culture, internet culture and consumerism.

The Fruit Man

From eating Fruit Pastilles on stage to sneaking a banana from a sporran – he's done both! – no other pop star on Earth seems to have as big an appetite for fruit as Harry. His habit of slipping fruit references into his songs has almost become a calling card, and fans love him for it.

THE FRUIT ERA

Fans sometimes call the first three albums of Harry's solo career – *Harry Styles*, *Fine Line* and *Harry's House* – his 'Fruit Era' because so many songs mention fruit. It is a playful idea, similar to the 'Cornetto Trilogy' of films by Edgar Wright, and beloved by Harry, starring Simon Pegg and Nick Frost, where each movie featured a Cornetto ice cream. With his fourth album, *Kiss All The Time. Disco, Occasionally.*, fans were excitedly wondering whether the fruit theme was still ripe for more references – but it looks like the era is over. *KISSCO* was sadly fruitless.

KIWI

Track seven from Harry's debut solo album, and a single in its own right, was the first song to reveal his obsession with fruit. Although the track is called **'Kiwi'**, neither the word nor the fruit actually appears in the lyrics. The song began as a joke with a silly working title, but the name ended up sticking. Harry has said it's one of his favourite songs.

'Kiwi' is the song Harry has performed live the most!

Harry Styles: Proudly meat-free since 2017.

WATERMELON SUGAR

This one's obvious! The song's anthemic chorus is stuffed with 26 mentions of the word watermelon and a few mentions of strawberries and berries, which supposedly taste like a summer evening, so wonderful and warm. Of course, it's not the only *Fine Line* track that has strawberries on its mind. On the third single, **'Adore You'**, Harry also references different fruits to describe the joy he feels when he's around a particular girl. He calls it a "strawberry-lipstick state of mind" and even throws in a line about lemons!

> "Never make eye contact with anyone while eating a banana."
>
> **Harry talks bananas.**

CHERRY

Another *Fine Line* track has a fruit in the title but never once mentions the little red fruit in the lyrics. That is probably because the song is not about fruit at all – it is about Harry's ex-girlfriend, Camille Rowe, and the cute word you get when you smush their names together: Cherry (or technically 'Charry'!). Harry wrote the song while feeling sad about their breakup.

GRAPEJUICE

A fan favourite on *Harry's House*, **'Grapejuice'** is not specifically about the fruit but about wine, and the effects of drinking a bottle of it – specifically a bottle of "rouge", as Harry sings, he is "so over white and pinks". On **'Little Freak'**, also from *Harry's House*, he mentions drinking "red wine and a ginger ale" but worries his date "would make fun" of him for it.

He's probably thinking about that breakfast, isn't he?

HARRY'S FOOD SONGS

1. Adore You
2. Watermelon Sugar
3. Music for a Sushi Restaurant
4. Grapejuice **5.** Cherry
6. Kiwi **7.** Keep Driving
8. Matilda **9.** Daylight
10. Little Freak
11. Satellite **12.** She

THE TOUR PITS

On Harry's *Love On Tour*, the 'Watermelon Pit' and 'Cherry Pit' were special areas for the audience right at the front of the stage. A 'pit' refers to a standing section closest to the stage. Lucky ticket holders in these spots get the best views of Harry, the loudest sound and the biggest chance of eye contact or waves from the legend himself. Fans who have these tickets are usually the ones with the signs they hope Harry will see, and the most likely to get an interaction with the man himself!

SLIP ON A KIWI

For years, Harry has had to deal with fans throwing things on stage while he performs, including flowers, Skittles, phones, stuffed toys, glow sticks and lots of handwritten notes. But one of the most unexpected moments happened at the start of *Live On Tour* in 2017 – a flying kiwi! During his two-night residency at London's Hammersmith Apollo, fans tossed kiwi fruits at the stage during the song **'Kiwi'**. One landed where he stepped, making him slip and nearly fall. He recovered quickly, but the message is clear: please don't throw things at Harry! Especially fruit. (Maybe eat it instead!)

WHY ALL THE FRUIT?

In 2019, Harry was asked why so many of his songs contain fruit references – he gave an answer that didn't really give fans the explanation they needed! "I don't know," he said. "They seem to be happening by accident, then when I kind of put the album together at the end, I realised there is a lot of fruit!"

Can't Get Enough

Going viral or becoming a trend – or even a meme – is something Harry does on a daily basis, whether he wants to or not! These are the memorable moments he wishes his fans would forget and the ones he'll remember forever ...

THE ONE WITH THE SPLIT PANTS

You have probably seen this moment online. On 26 January, 2023, during a Los Angeles concert at the Kia Forum, Harry hilariously split his tan leather trousers at the seams when he dropped to his knees to perform **'Music for a Sushi Restaurant'**. He quickly grabbed a pride flag to cover up and kept singing like a pro. *Friends* Actress Jennifer Aniston (and celebrity crush!) was in the audience and was seen laughing. Harry apologised to fans in the front row, joking, "My trousers ripped. I feel I must apologise to a certain few of you right down in the front there. I promise it's not part of the show ... It's a family show … or is it? It is. Or is it?'"

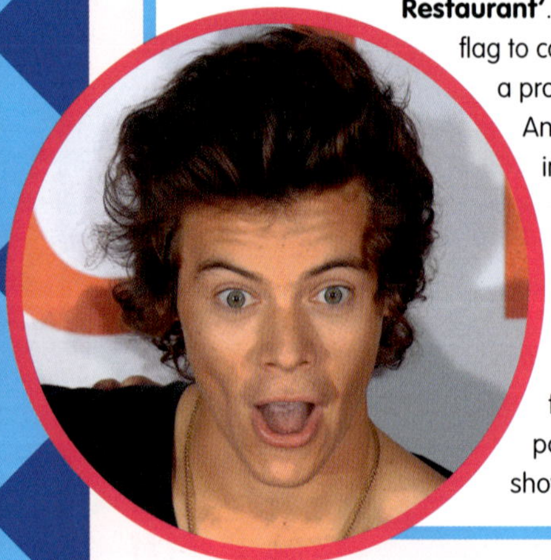

A DECENT PROPOSAL

Everyone knows how wholesome a Harry Styles concert is, but once in a while he outdoes even himself. In Lisbon, Portugal, in 2023, during *Love On Tour*, he paused the show to help with an adorable marriage proposal that quickly went viral. After spotting a couple with a sign, he leaned over the barrier and handed the man his microphone. He serenaded his girlfriend with Elvis Presley's **'Can't Help Falling in Love'** before proposing on one knee. Thankfully, she said yes. There were at least four proposals during that tour alone!

HELLO, HARRIES!

Just as famous as the colourful feather boas on *Love On Tour* were Harry's playful and wholesome crowd interactions – frequent moments where he stopped mid-show to read fan signs and speak directly to the audience. The tour had plenty of standout moments, including pausing a show to thank his first schoolteacher, helping a fan come out to their parents, throwing flowers to a young fan, and stopping a gig so a fan could propose, prompting the response: "I have been out for an hour. You have been here for 15 seconds and have stolen the entire show," he joked to the happy couple.

SPILL YOUR GUTS OR FILL YOUR GUTS

In 2020, Harry played a game called 'Spill Your Guts', with former girlfriend Kendall Jenner, on *The Late Late Show with James Corden*. In the game, players must either answer an embarrassing question or eat something disgusting. The menu included bug trifle, jellyfish, giant water scorpion, cow blood, pork tongue jelly and salmon smoothie, yuck! Kendall asked which songs on *Fine Line* were written about her and which One Direction member's solo album he liked the most. Harry refused to answer both questions, eating a giant water scorpion as punishment. Gross.

MR WORLDWIDE HANDSOME

In 2017, researchers at the Centre for Advanced Facial Cosmetic and Plastic Surgery used the Golden Ratio, a mathematical formula, to analyse the symmetry and beauty of the faces of male celebrities. Harry scored the highest on two features: his eyes and his chin. His eyes measured 98.15 per cent of the 'perfect' ratio, while his chin scored an incredible 99.7 per cent. Overall, he ranked fourth most attractive man in the world, behind George Clooney, Bradley Cooper and Brad Pitt. Finally, the scientific proof we needed to justify our love for him!

"I think I was always just a show-off. I say that like it's past tense."

Harry on being a show-off.

Harry sparkling and shining at the BRIT Awards, 2023.

Live Life Out Loud

Harry is anything but, ahem, one-directional – he contains multitudes! He is a man in love with the world and all the extraordinary things he can do in it. Life is short, so Harry is squeezing as much fun from it as possible ...

CAN YOU CATCH 'STED SARANDOS'?

In his downtime, Harry loves to run – and, naturally, he's very good at it! In 2025, he completed the Tokyo and Berlin Marathons, two of the world's biggest races. In Berlin, he finished in 2 hours, 59 minutes – pretty astonishing for a non-professional runner. Harry took up running after turning 30 to give his life structure when not on tour and to prove he could do something tough on his own. He had dreamed of running a marathon in his twenties but didn't train properly back then. He ran under the secret name 'Sted Sarandos' – Sted from Styles and Edward (his middle name), with Sarandos borrowed from Netflix boss Ted Sarandos – though no-one is quite sure why!

GET LEGS!

Alongside Harry's love of watching and playing football, the singer also enjoys golf as a way to relax. He often plays at Sunningdale Golf Club in Berkshire, where he is a member. He is said to be pretty good, with a handicap of 13, which is considered above average for an amateur golfer.

UNITED FOREVER

Harry is a known fan of Manchester United. The singer, who grew up in Cheshire, has supported the Red Devils since childhood and has been spotted attending their matches in his downtime. He has previously cited David Beckham and the famous 'Class of 1992' era as major sporting inspirations.

AVID READER

We imagine that it would make Harry very happy that you are reading this book because he is an avid reader himself, often choosing books that explore themes of love, art and philosophy. His favourite authors are Haruki Murakami and Alain de Botton.

CURATING A MELTDOWN

As if he was not busy enough in 2026, Harry Styles was also hand-picked to curate London's famous 10-day *Meltdown Festival* in June at the Southbank Centre, part of the venue's 75th anniversary celebrations. As curator, he will choose the artists, performances and events across the multi-arts festival while preparing for his record-breaking Wembley Stadium shows just over the river. "I am deeply honoured. My goal as the curator is to share the music and art that I love, and to celebrate the rich history of the venue," he said.

TAKE THE PLUNGE!

Every day, as part of his wellbeing and fitness routine, Harry plunges into an ice-cold bath and practises meditation – he has shared photos of himself sitting in icy water. Cold water is thought to help muscles recover after exercise and boost your mood. He also enjoys cold-water swimming, often at the Men's Bathing Pond on Hampstead Heath near his home. "A swim – it's the one thing you never regret," he has said.

TATTOOS

Much has been written about Harry's 60-plus tattoos. His first was a simple outline of a star, but his most iconic is the large butterfly across his chest, inked in 2013. Harry has admitted that some of his tattoos are a bit "stupid," possibly referring to the time he got "Late Late Show" tattooed on himself live on *The Late Late Show with James Corden*.

The Golden Boy meets his fans, and, er, their mobile phones!

Harry's House

Welcome to *Harry's House*! This is the moment Harry arrived as the world's greatest cultural phenomenon. Come on in, make yourself at home.

The night that Harry became a serious *contender*!!

HOME SWEET HOME

Released on May 20, 2022, Harry's third solo album, *Harry's House*, was an immediate global hit. Filled with songs about mindfulness, love and joy, it has become Harry's calling card and the defining statement of 'Poptimism', the singer's signature brand of positive pop. The title was inspired by one of the most influential musicians in Japanese pop, Haruomi Hosono, and his 1973 album *Hosono House*, which Harry was listening to a lot at the time of recording. Harry borrowed the title because he originally wanted to make a simple, intimate acoustic EP in his house, but changed course when the pandemic hit, reframing the concept of 'home' as a state of mind rather than a specific place.

MUSIC FOR A SUSHI RESTAURANT

With its now-iconic music video, in which Harry plays a sushi chef – but quickly transforms into a half-human, half-fish creature! – **'Music For A Sushi Restaurant'**, the opening track of *Harry's House*, fast became a fan favourite. The song's creation came from one night when Harry Styles was in a sushi restaurant in Los Angeles with his producer and one of his songs from his second album, *Fine Line*, came on. Harry told his companion, "This is really strange music for a sushi restaurant!" That sentence gave him the idea for a "really fun album title" that eventually blossomed into the song's title. Imagine if Harry had never gone to that restaurant – we'd never have the song!

THE UPSIDE-DOWN

The surreal cover image of *Harry's House*, photographed by Hanna Moon, features Harry looking pensively down at the floor – or is it the ceiling? – of an upside-down room decorated sparsely with furniture. The empty room represents Harry's inner world rather than a literal home. As Harry's said, the album is about "a day in my house" and "a day in my mind" – the cover visualises that mental space. The fact that it's upside-down is very revealing!

RECORD-BREAKER

As you know, *Harry's House* gave the world four incredible singles: **'As It Was'**, **'Late Night Talking'**, **'Music for a Sushi Restaurant'** and **'Matilda'**. But did you know that, as a result, all four songs were concurrently in the top 10 of the Billboard Hot 100, making Harry Styles the first – and only – British solo artist to achieve this feat.

5 FEBRUARY 2023

The night Harry's life changed forever: a.k.a. when he won Album of the Year at the 65th Grammy Awards in Los Angeles! Some might have said he was an unlikely contender, since the category was stacked against him: Adele, Beyoncé, Bad Bunny, ABBA, Kendrick Lamar and Coldplay, but we think it just shows how strong the album is. The Recording Academy (made up of peers in the music industry, who determine the Grammy winners) obviously thought so too!

FOUR MILLION

Harry's House was both the fastest-selling and best-selling album of 2022 worldwide, with more than four million copies sold in that year alone, outselling former-squeeze, Taylor Swift. The album was so well received that America's most prestigious music magazine, *Rolling Stone*, ranked it as the 67th greatest album of the 21st century in 2025 and placed it at number 491 in its list of the 500 greatest albums of all time.

AN ODE TO Ms. WORMWOOD

Harry Wormwood, the father of the magical Matilda in Roald Dahl's beloved children's book, *Matilda*, is not the only Harry in Matilda's life. The seventh track on Harry's House, **'Matilda'**, was inspired by the book and its famous character. Harry wanted to write a song about the fictional five-year-old, asking himself the question: "If I were speaking to Matilda now that she's grown up, who's been mistreated by her family, how would you speak to her?" The song is one of Harry's personal favourites and one that means the most to him. When he first played it for a couple of his friends, they cried. It was then that he realised the song was extra special.

Harry sends fans into a frenzy by wearing one of his iconic jumpsuits for his performance on *The Today Show*, NYC, 2022.

"It doesn't feel like my life is over if this album isn't a commercial success. I just want to make music that is fun in terms of the process - that I can be proud of for a long time. That my friends can be proud of, that my family can be proud of - and that my kids will be proud of one day."

Forget those sales targets! Harry has discovered that making music for the pure joy of it is enough for him.

TRACK LIST

1. Music for a Sushi Restaurant
2. Late Night Talking
3. Grapejuice **4.** As It Was
5. Daylight **6.** Little Freak
7. Matilda **8.** Cinema
9. Daydreaming
10. Keep Driving **11.** Satellite
12. Boyfriends
13. Love of My Life

As It Was

Harry's biggest hit was actually the last song written for *Harry's House*, and the one he knew was destined to be huge. "This is the one. I'm telling you!" he said. How right he was ...

> After everything that's happened over the last two and half, three years, I think the sentiment of 'it's not the same as it was' felt pretty perfect.
>
> **Harry about 'As It Was'.**

NUMBER ONE TWICE

Harry joined a very exclusive club of superstars when his film *Don't Worry Darling* hit No. 1 at the box office on 25 September, 2022 while his song **'As It Was'** was also No. 1 on the Billboard Hot 100. Only a few artists have achieved this double success at the same time, including Prince, Eminem and Beyoncé, who all starred in their own hit films while topping the charts with their own songs (*Purple Rain*, *8 Mile* and *Dreamgirls*, respectively).

"COME ON, HARRY, WE WANT TO SAY GOODNIGHT TO YOU!"

The (very adorable) child's voice at the beginning of **'As It Was'** belongs to Harry's goddaughter, Ruby Winston, the young daughter of British producer Ben Winston. Ruby used to call Harry before bed each night, but one evening when he missed Ruby's call, she left him the (now) iconic voicemail telling him she was not happy! In the studio, Harry dug out the message and used it to open the song. "I loved it so it stuck and I hope when she's older, she will enjoy looking back on it," he said.

FIRST PERFORMANCE

Harry performed **'As It Was'** live for the first time ever on 15 April, 2022 during his headlining set at the *Coachella Festival* in California. He also debuted two other *Harry's House* songs to the lucky crowd that night, **'Boyfriends'** and **'Late Night Talking'**. After the show, Harry admitted the reaction to the song overwhelmed him. "We came offstage … I just needed a minute … I wasn't sure what it was. Just that the energy felt insane." Even after One Direction's huge fame, this moment still felt completely new. He knew something had changed.

FOUR BILLION CLUB

'As It Was' is now one of the biggest streaming hits ever. It was played more than 16 million times worldwide on Spotify on its first day – a Guinness World Record. Within a year, it had reached 1.5 billion plays and spent ten weeks at No. 1 in the UK and 15 weeks at No. 1 on the US Billboard Hot 100, another record. Today, it has more than four billion Spotify streams, joining only a few songs such as The Weeknd's **'Blinding Lights'**, Ed Sheeran's **'Shape of You'**, Lewis Capaldi's **'Someone You Loved'** and Drake's **'One Dance'**.

Greatest music video ever!

HEAD TO THE PENGUIN POOL!

Ukrainian filmmaker Tanu Muino directed the now-legendary video – which passed a billion views in April 2026. It shows Harry in a sparkly red jumpsuit spinning with a former lover on a moving platform before she is pulled away, symbolising being stuck in a relationship and needing change. The video was filmed at London's Barbican Centre, the Royal Horticultural Halls and the Penguin Pool at London Zoo – you know the bit! It won Best Pop and Best Cinematography at the 2022 MTV VMAs.

During *Love On Tour*, in the bridge of **'As It Was'**, many European fans began shouting "Leave America!" at the top of their lungs when Harry sings that part. It was meant as a playful message asking him to stop spending so much time in the US (where he lives).

THE SONG THAT BROKE THE INTERNET

'As It Was' became Harry's most award-winning song ever. It won Favourite Pop Song at the 2022 American Music Awards, where he also picked up Favourite Male Pop Artist. In 2023, he performed it at the Grammys, where *Harry's House* won Album of the Year. It won Song of the Year at the 2023 BRIT Awards – his third BRITs win in that category – and was named the most-performed song of the year at the Ivor Novello Awards.

FROM HARRY'S HEART

While Harry often works with a trusted team of collaborators, he was the mastermind behind this track. The famous 'dah, dah, dah' synth line came from Harry sitting at a Moog (a synthesizer) and writing both the melody and lyrics. While working on the second verse, he even began referring to himself in the third person – a very unusual move for a pop song! "So much of this song just came from Harry's heart," said producer Tyler Johnson, who was there when it was created.

His future's so bright, we're gonna need some sunglasses!

Love On Tour!

Following 2017's *Live on Tour*, Harry's second 173-date, 22-month world adventure, *Love On Tour* sold out in less than 30 minutes. Were YOU there?

SET LIST

***Love On Tour* 2021–23**

Daydreaming, Golden, Adore You, Keep Driving, Stockholm Syndrome, She, Matilda, Satellite, Late Night Talking, Cinema, Music For A Sushi Restaurant, Treat People With Kindness, What Makes You Beautiful, Grapejuice, Watermelon Sugar, Fine Line, Sign Of The Times, As It Was, Kiwi.

BIG BOA ENERGY!

Sequins. Handmade signs. Pride flags. Pink cowboy hats. Harry's *Love On Tour* was the definitive global jaunt made with fans in mind. From the up-close-and-personal stage design to the all-girl band, the tour was a full-blown tour de force of Harry-mania. But what was the most memorable item of all? Feather boas, of course! Harry first wore these fluffy fashion accessories – three, to be precise! – at the Grammy Awards in March 2021, and ever since, they have become uniquely associated with him. His purple feather boa was the hit look of the night. According to a global fashion shopping platform, page views for feather boas saw a massive 1,500 per cent spike in the 48 hours following the awards show! Since then, fans have adopted feather boas as their unofficial tour uniform.

We have all the love for these VIP passes!

We all boa down to Harry's iconic style ...

Hats and sunglasses and pink feathers, oh my!

FIVE MILLION FANS

A landmark moment in modern pop touring, *Love On Tour* spanned five continents and saw Harry sparkle and shine for more than five million fans worldwide. The tour was celebrated for its inclusive atmosphere and became a true cultural phenomenon. It also made history, becoming the fifth highest-grossing tour of all time, and won Tour of the Year at the iHeartRadio Music Awards in 2023.

There's a fine line between love and obsession. Amirite?

WELCOME TO WEMBLEY

In June 2023, Harry Styles made history with six sold-out nights at London's Wembley Stadium. Playing to a total of more than 500,000 fans, the run was a career-defining moment. At the time, it set a record for the most shows played by a solo artist at Wembley Stadium (a record beaten by Taylor Swift a year later, and then broken *again* by Harry on his *Together, Together* tour). On the first night, a clearly overwhelmed Harry said hello to this history-making moment: "Good evening, wonderful people of Wembley … and the surrounding areas … this place is very special to me. Are we all feeling emotionally stable? Please feel free to be whoever it is you've always wanted to be tonight."

SHOUT OUT TO MITCH!

One of our favourite moments during the Love On Tour was when Harry faked being angry when a fan kept looking at Mitch Rowland – Harry's guitarist and songwriter – during a performance. Spotting it, Harry pretended to get angry, saying, "Look at me! This is about me!"

WHO THREW THE NUGGET?

Harry follows a pescatarian diet, a largely vegetarian way of eating that includes fish and seafood, but no other meat. In 2022, during a show at Madison Square Garden, a fan threw chicken nuggets onstage, prompting the crowd to start chanting he should eat one. Harry laughed it off, saying, "I don't eat chicken, sorry. I don't eat meat." The moment earned him PETA's 2022 Best Viral Moment for Animals Award.

END WITH A BEGINNING

A show now beloved by fans worldwide is the poignant closing concert of his Love On Tour on 22 July 2023 in Reggio Emilia, Italy, where he performed to more than 100,000 fans at the RCF Arena. The emotional finale of the historic tour featured a surprise: a new eight-minute piano ballad titled 'Forever, Forever', with a video. The video included the teaser "We Belong Together", now known as the chorus to 'Aperture', and was widely seen as Harry teeing up his next era for Kiss All The Time. Disco, Occasionally. Before playing the song, Harry told the crowd in Italian, "I wrote this for you" and then vanished. It remains the only live performance of the song.

Harry For The Win

> I wanna thank my family for being the most supportive, understanding, patient family. I wanna thank my mum for signing me up for *The X Factor* without asking me. I also wanna thank Niall, Louis, Liam and Zayn. I wouldn't be here without them.

Harry's BRIT Awards 2023 speech.

Harry has won more than 100 major awards since he started his solo career in 2016. Most of them celebrate how amazing he is ... but some are just plain weird!

SEXIEST MUSICIAN ALIVE

Perhaps the most spot-on award win ever … In 2024, America's *People* magazine named Harry the Sexiest Musician Alive after nearly 350,000 reader votes were cast in a highly competitive poll. He beat Shaboozey and Zach Bryan to the crown. In 2013, he won the British Style Award, beating David Beckham, Kate Moss, the Duchess of Cambridge and Cara Delevingne. The award recognises the person who best represents London's global fashion influence. Accepting the award, Harry simply said, "This is very, very kind."

Winner Winner Tofu Dinner!

A NIGHT OF FOUR

At the 2023 BRIT Awards in London on 11 February, 2023, Harry dominated the night, winning four major prizes. He took home Artist of the Year, Album of the Year for *Harry's House*, Song of the Year for **'As It Was'**, and Best Pop/R&B Act. One of the funniest moments, however, involved Lewis Capaldi. When Harry presented him with an award, the two shared a cheeky kiss on the lips, sending the crowd wild. Harry celebrated the only way he knows how – with style. Afterwards, Lewis joked, "I just kissed Harry Styles on the lips!"

VILLAIN OF THE YEAR

At the 2014 *NME* Awards – infamous for their sarcastic, tongue-in-cheek categories – Harry was crowned Villain of the Year. The title is meant as a joke rather than a real insult, and past winners have included politicians and controversial celebrities. Harry beat a list of serious (and very un-villain-like) contenders, proving how obsessed the world's press was with him at the time. He took the whole thing in good humour, saying afterwards, "Gotta take the rough with the smooth, eh?"

BEST NIGHT EVER

When Harry won Album of the Year for *Harry's House* at the 65th Grammy Awards in Los Angeles he was visibly shocked. Harry's acceptance speech went like this: "On nights like tonight, it's obviously so important for us to remember that there is no such thing as 'best' in music. I don't think any of us sit in the studio making decisions based on what is going to get us one of these. This is really, really kind. I'm so, so grateful. This doesn't happen to people like me very often."

FIRST MUSICAL AWARD

Formed with school friends at Holmes Chapel Comprehensive School, the four-piece White Eskimo featured Harry on vocals alongside Will Sweeny (drums), Nick Clough (bass) and Haydn Morris (guitar). Amazingly, they had only been playing together for about two weeks when they entered their school's Battle of the Bands around 2009–2010 – and won! Performing covers of **'Are You Gonna Be My Girl'** and **'Summer of '69'**, they scooped £100 and a headline slot at the local Goosfest Cheshire festival. It all started here ...

WORLD'S BEST SMILE

It's official! What we've known in our hearts all along has now been scientifically proven to be in true. In 2023, Harry was crowned the celebrity with the world's most incredible smile by leading dentists, who praised the symmetry and shape of his teeth. Experts said his front teeth are slightly longer, creating a balanced, eye-catching look that works perfectly with his symmetrical face. Agreed.

FIRST EVER AWARD

Harry's first ever music award was One Direction's first major award at the 2012 BRIT Award for Best British Single for their debut hit, **'What Makes You Beautiful'**, on 21 February, 2012. It marked the first of seven BRIT Awards the group won. Harry said: "This win shows how good all our fans are."

Suited up for the 1D boys' first ever win.

You and I

Harry is a man with many famous friends (and several famous ex-girlfriends). These friendships have given Harry the support he's needed to ensure fame never swallowed him whole.

GEMMA STYLES

Harry loves his big sister Gemma, who is three years older than him. Gemma is often seen at his shows cheering from the sidelines. Harry has said she helped keep him grounded when life changed overnight. Gemma published her debut book *Why Am I Like This?* in 2023 and hosts the podcast *Good Influence*, which explores how social media shapes our lives. "It's a strange experience having your baby brother run off and become a pop star!" Gemma has said.

HIS BAND

Harry is close to his touring band, many of whom have performed with him for years and will return for the *Together, Together* tour. Since April 2017, acclaimed drummer and backing vocalist Sarah Jones has been a key part of his live sound. She is married to guitarist Mitch Rowland, one of Harry's most trusted musical collaborators. Jones and Rowland actually met while rehearsing for *Live on Tour*.

THE DREAM TEAM

Harry has three trusted collaborators, known as his dream team. Kid Harpoon (Tom Hull) is his long-time co-writer and producer. He also produced Miley Cyrus's massive 2024 single **'Flowers'**. Guitarist Mitch Rowland has been by Harry's side since his debut album and co-writes much of his music too. And Tyler Johnson is Harry's trusted producer and songwriter, who also wrote a few tracks on Beyoncé's 2024 album, *Cowboy Carter*.

The golden boy with his dream team.

TEN YEARS ON

Still thinking about his BFFs! To mark One Direction's 10th anniversary on 23 July, 2020, Harry shared a heartfelt message on Instagram reflecting his former band's incredible journey and how much they still mean to him. "I've been struggling to put into words how grateful I am for everything that's happened over the last ten years. I've seen things and places that I'd only ever dreamt of … To all the fans, I love you … You did it all, and you changed everything. And finally … to the boys, I love you."

TAYLOR SWIFT

Harry's three-month 'romance' with Taylor Swift may be ancient history, but fans still can't get enough of it. When two of the biggest pop stars on the planet date, it must be love, right? Not quite. Their famous second date – a stroll through New York's Central Park in 2012 – was photographed and printed in papers all over the world. Looking back, Harry said, "When I see photos from that day, I think relationships are hard, at any age … It was a learning experience for sure … I just wanted it to be a normal date." If they ever released a song together, the Internet would probably explode! (It could happen.)

ED SHEERAN

Harry and Ed, who used to write for One Direction (**'Little Things'**, **'18'**, **'Moments'** and **'Over Again'**) are close friends. They even share a friendship tattoo – a Pingu one! In 2015, Ed said he no longer needed to write for One Direction because they had become strong songwriters themselves. Ed has always spoken warmly about Harry. "We were in LA and he had a day off," Ed recalled. "He spent £3,000 on pizza and drove around giving them out to homeless people. He's a pretty genuine guy."

> I feel like when people label people as famous, they take away a lot of substance that they have as a person.
>
> **Harry on fame.**

JAMES CORDEN

A superstar in America in his own right thanks to *The Late Late Show*, British comedian James Corden has been a close friend of Harry's since Ben Winston (James's producer) directed One Direction's music videos **'Best Song Ever'**, **'Story of My Life'**, **'Midnight Memories'** and **'You & I'**. Harry became a frequent – and hilarious – guest on James's show and even took up a special week-long residency to promote his debut solo album *Harry Styles* in June 2017. Harry's edition of *Carpool Karaoke*, with Harry interviewing James instead of the other way round, was also a viral sensation.

BEN WINSTON

Twelve years Harry's senior, TV producer Ben Winston gave Harry a place to stay during the early whirlwind of fame. Living with Ben's family helped keep Harry grounded as the world around him spun out of control. For the first two years of his career, Harry slept on a mattress in the attic of their Hampstead Heath home. "No one ever found out," Winston said. "He made our house a home. And when he moved out, we were gutted". Harry is godfather to Winston's daughter Ruby, whose voice so famously cues up **'As It Was'**.

TOMO CAMPBELL

With fans including Harry and Alexa Chung, Tomo Campbell is one of the hottest young artists in Britain today and a rising star of London's creative scene. Tomo is married to Sam Teasdale, twin sister of Lou Teasdale, the famed One Direction hairstylist known to fans worldwide. Tomo and Harry have been friends for years after meeting when Harry bought one of Tomo's colourful abstract works. In summer 2020, Harry reportedly spent months travelling through France and Italy on a road trip with the artist, a journey that greatly inspired Harry creatively.

He Can Sing Anything!

As a child, Harry loved to sing covers on a karaoke machine given to him by his grandfather. Today, nothing has changed! Harry frequently loves to perform unique versions of rock and pop classics, reinterpreting them to make them his own. There are loads to choose from, but these are considered his very best ...

'JUICE'

Harry loves Lizzo – and fans definitely know it! Their musical love affair began when Harry covered Lizzo's hit **'Juice'** on BBC Radio 1's *Live Lounge*. The performance went viral, not just because it sounded great but because nobody expected him to sing it. Harry later praised her, saying, "She's exactly what you want an artist to be, which is themselves." Lizzo returned the favour with a powerful cover of Harry's **'Adore You'**, calling him "her favourite British import". They've been BFFs ever since.

'BIG YELLOW TAXI'

For a special Valentine's Day morning show, Harry and his band covered Joni Mitchell's **'Big Yellow Taxi'** live on BBC Radio 2's *The Zoe Ball Show*. It's one of his favourite songs by one of his favourite songwriters, the legendary 1970s icon Joni Mitchell, who influenced his early solo work. The classic is known for its environmental message – and Harry is a sustainability champion – but the live recording shows how much fun he's having. He even lets out a little squeal and flashes a huge smile at the end. Check it out!

'TOXIC'

While touring the US, Harry played a Halloween show during his 20-date Madison Square Garden residency on 31 October, 2021. The show was titled *Harry's Harryween Fancy Dress Party*, and Harry and his fans fully embraced the dress-up theme. During the show, Harry wore a Pennywise-inspired clown costume and performed a cover of Britney Spears's classic **'Toxic'**, which sent the crowd crazy! It was WILD.

Harry has always been pretty in pink.

'MAN! I FEEL LIKE A WOMAN!'

"This lady taught me to sing," Harry told the crowd when he brought country superstar Shania Twain on stage at his *Coachella* headline appearance in 2022, explaining he grew up singing her songs in the car with his mum. After performing **'Man! I Feel Like a Woman!'** and **'You're Still the One'**, he joked, "She also taught me that men are trash!" sending Twain into fits of laughter. Harry later called touring with her a "full circle" moment – and was so inspired that he invited her to join his 2026 *Together, Together* tour.

> The moment you feel more comfortable with yourself, everything becomes a lot easier.
>
> **Harry on Harry.**

'THE CHAIN'

Excluding One Direction songs, this Fleetwood Mac classic is Harry's most cherished – and most performed – cover, which he has played nearly 90 times. He first performed it at BBC Radio 1's *Live Lounge* in 2017, shortly after releasing his debut solo album. The song's writer, Stevie Nicks, is also a close friend of Harry's and one of his biggest supporters. "When Harry came into our lives, I said, 'Oh my God, this is the son I never had,'" Stevie once famously said. Aw!

'SLEDGEHAMMER'

In March 2020, Harry Styles stopped by *The Howard Stern Show* to perform a lively cover of Peter Gabriel's 1986 anthem **'Sledgehammer'** – one of the decade's biggest hits, famous for its groundbreaking, brain-melting music video. During his interview with host, Howard Stern, Harry revealed that much of his *Fine Line* album had been recorded at Gabriel's Real World Studios near Bath. Harry revealed he has had a long-time admiration for Gabriel's production work. Harry's performance of **'Sledgehammer'** impressed the rock legend so much that Gabriel later shared the clip with a pair of clapping hand emojis – a rare seal of approval from the notoriously private singer.

Endlessly Infinite

Numbers are hugely important to Harry, both personally and as a way of measuring just how successful he is. Get your fingers ready to count, because these figures are anything but by-the-numbers ...

$617,300,000

That's the staggering total gross of Harry's *Love On Tour* (2021–23), making it the ninth highest-grossing tour of *all time* (behind acts like Taylor Swift, Coldplay and Ed Sheeran). Across 173 shows worldwide, more than five million tickets were sold!

2

The number two has an extra-special significance in Harry's life. He was born in the second month, February (on the 1st). His biggest album era peaked in 2022, and his massive *Love On Tour* lasted 22 months, finally ending on 22 July, 2023. Even his finances follow the pattern – as of 2025, his estimated net worth is around £225 million!

586-533-5477

A US phone number used by Harry Styles Headquarters (HSHQ) as a fan hotline. If you dial it, you don't reach Harry himself – you hear a pre-recorded message connected to current promotions, announcements or tour campaigns. In January 2026, it began to play cryptic teasers and fun, clue-based messages tied to album *Kiss All The Time. Disco, Occasionally.* *(Warning: Don't dial this number without permission from an adult!)*

"There's hundreds and thousands, if not millions, of musicians who are so far superior to me. When I look at it, there's no reason for it to have been me who got to do this for a living."

Harry on the odds of him being a famous musician.

4

The number of UK hit singles Harry has had during his solo career – so far. Harry's debut single **'Sign of the Times'** soared to the top of the charts in 2017. Then he peaked again with **'As It Was'** in 2022, before scoring a double in 2026 with the first two singles from new album KISSCO: **'Aperture'** and **'American Girls'**.

26,800,000,000

The total Spotify streams Harry has amassed as of March 2026 – powered by around 65 million monthly listeners. This makes him a top-tier force on the platform, consistently ranking among the Top 50 most-streamed artists worldwide.

17

The number 17 is tattooed on Harry's collarbone – but it isn't his lucky number. Ironically, it comes from an unlucky moment. In the early days of One Direction, Harry reportedly lost money while gambling in Australia after betting on "17 black" at a roulette table. Instead of forgetting the loss, he chose to mark it permanently on his skin. Interestingly, James Bond also bets on 17 black in *Diamonds Are Forever* – are the two related?

5.11

Running at a lengthy 5 minutes and 11 seconds, **'Aperture'** is Harry's longest song to reach No. 1 in the UK and the longest song to hit the top of the UK charts in the 2020s decade so far. At a time when most hit songs are getting shorter for streaming success, **'Aperture'** bucked the trend!

270,000

Harry is one of the most written-about celebrities on fan-fiction site Wattpad, where there are more than 270,000 stories featuring him as a character. These range from sweet romances to wild adventures and alternate universes, proof of just how big and creative his fandom is. For many young writers, Harry is an inspiration for storytelling. Olivia Rodrigo used to write One Direction fan fiction when she was in elementary school. Many of these works of fan fiction have been published – and one has even been made into a film!

100,000

Harry drew his largest-ever audience during his headline performance at *Coachella* 2022, with more than 100,000 fans packed in front of the California festival's main stage in April. As the first (and so far only) former One Direction member to headline the iconic event, he delivered a career-defining show. The festival was completely sold out and has an official capacity of around 125,000 people – so you do the maths!

Just Perfect

Harry has many favourite things and surprising little obsessions. Here's a peek inside the likes, loves and must-haves that make Harry unmistakably Harry ...

MAKING A FOOL OF HIMSELF

In November 2019, Harry was the host and musical guest on *Saturday Night Live*, fully embracing one of his favourite things – being silly. He threw himself into bizarre sketches, goofy characters – his performance as Doug the Chihuahua was insanely good! – and self-deprecating jokes, clearly loving every second. One standout moment came during his monologue when he teased a One Direction reunion. "I was in a band called One Direction," he said. "How crazy would it be if they were here tonight?" After a long pause, he added dryly, "Well, they're not." Millions of hearts broke.

LOVING HIS FANS

Harry's love for his fans is one of his favourite things, and few stories show it better than his bond with 78-year-old Canadian superfan and great-grandmother Reina Lafantaisie, nicknamed "Grammy Granny." After going viral for her devotion to Harry, she was invited to the 2023 Grammy Awards ceremony, where she announced Harry as winner of Album of the Year and shared a heartfelt hug on stage. Reina later called him "the most caring, humble, and down-to-earth person". The entire evening was a dream come true for Reina – and Harry too.

LOOKING GOOD

Gucci is widely considered Harry's favourite fashion brand and his relationship with the label goes back years. In 2018 he officially became the face of Gucci, fronting campaigns designed by his close friend, creative director Alessandro Michele. One of his most famous Gucci looks came at the 2022 Venice Film Festival premiere of *Don't Worry Darling*, where he wore a navy suit with a plunging open collar, a strikingly sophisticated look.

Harry's greatest Gucci moment?

BEING KIND

Kindness is one of Harry's defining traits, and fans see it at his shows all the time. During a 2023 concert in Cardiff, he paused the entire performance so a pregnant fan could use the bathroom – promising she wouldn't miss a thing. While she was gone, he entertained the crowd, then helped her choose a name for her baby when she returned. The heart-warming moment went viral with one fan on TikTok writing, "How can one person be so frickin' awesome!"

FAVOURITE ALL-TIME MOMENT

In a career filled with highlights, how can anyone choose just one? They can't. But there is one moment that sticks out as Harry's all-time favourite moment. We'll let Harry tell it: "For me it was the jumpsuit with the red hearts and the white T-shirt underneath that I wore at Wembley Stadium. When you move at such a fast pace there's always the question of, 'Am I enjoying this enough?' During that show, that fear left my body and there was a sense of calm. I could see my parents dancing together and, in the encore, when we played **'Sign of the Times'**, it started raining and it was as though we'd paid for the rain. It was perfect timing. I remember having a massive smile on my face. I thought, 'How can I ask for any more joy?' I felt so full in that moment. I felt like I was flying."

> I don't think you can ever get used to being this famous.
>
> **Harry on his level of fame.**

TELLING DAD JOKES

Harry's love of dad jokes is legendary. He's told lots over the years – too many! Who knows what jokes he will share with us in the future. These are his favourites:

What did Zero say to Eight?
Nice belt!

Knock knock.
Who's there?
Hula.
Hula who?
P.*
Done with a finger-cheek pop!

Knock knock.
Who's there?
A cow goes.
A cow goes who?
No, a cow goes MOO!

CLASSIC HARRY

Winning a prestigious award is a huge accomplishment in any artist's career – a moment no one wants to miss. Yet at the 2014 BRIT Awards, when One Direction were called onstage to accept the Global Success Award, he nearly did miss it! Mid-speech, Harry suddenly came sprinting through the audience and up onto the stage, to the crowd's delight. So where was he? Backstage … in the toilet. Yes, Harry nearly missed one of the band's biggest awards because he needed a wee.

Kiss All the Time. Disco, Occasionally.

6 March, 2026 was a huge day for Harry. It was the day the singer's fourth album, *Kiss All the Time. Disco, Occasionally.*, finally arrived, six weeks after it was first teased with cryptic 'WE BELONG TOGETHER' posters all over the world.

BOWIE'S BERLIN

With his long-trusted collaborators Kid Harpoon and Tyler Johnson, Harry moved to Berlin for the first few months of the album's production – a bold move inspired by his idol David Bowie. It was here in the 1970s that Bowie escaped global fame and discovered the thrill of electronic music – and total creative freedom. Harry's upbeat rhythm for the album's signature sound was inspired by the famous Berlin club scene that he enjoyed while making the album. Harry took a big creative risk to sound unlike anything he'd done before, making 12 songs bursting with a brand-new synth, electro and dance energy. "I wanted to recreate what I felt on the dance floor, being lost in the instrumentation and the musicality," he said of its sound.

'APERTURE' OPENS

Harry's first single in three years, **'Aperture'** was released on 23 January, 2026. It immediately smashed records with 13.2 million first-day streams on Spotify, becoming the biggest opening ever for a solo male artist on the platform! The song may be Track 1 on the album, but it was actually the last one written, finished when Harry was feeling his most free and simply having fun with the music. He chose it as the lead single to set fans' expectations – something radically new, yet with its anthemic "We Belong Together" chorus, totally Harry.

KATTDO CAN DO

Within its first day of being released into the world, *KATTDO* smashed global streaming records with more than 63 million streams in its first 24 hours – making it the biggest album of 2026 at the time of its release.

GO KISSCO CRAZY!

When Harry announced the album's title in January 2026, the world went crazy – mostly because no one knew what it meant! At first, fans shortened the long name to its acronym: *KATTDO*, before it quickly became lovingly known as *KISSCO*. The nickname blended the album's two big themes – love and music – and was inspired by Harry noticing how Italians seemed to kiss all the time while he was living in Italy. For Harry, the title became a "life mantra" about remembering to pause and have fun. As he joked: "It's unhealthy to disco all the time!"

STYLISH ON SNL

One of the biggest promos for the album came on 14 March, 2026, when Harry returned as both host and musical guest on the iconic New York sketch comedy show *Saturday Night Live* – the second time he has pulled double duty. A week earlier, Harry was in the audience watching Ryan Gosling host "to get a feel for things". When Ryan pointed out that the cameras were only focusing on Harry, the actor joked: "Harry, your coolness is becoming an issue."

Harry's music video got off to a flying start.

POP UP & PARTY

From London to Tokyo, sixteen pop-up shops celebrating the album drop opened on 6 March 2026 across seven countries. Thousands of fans queued to buy exclusive *KISSCO* merch – no doubt to wear on tour! Alongside the pop-ups, Harry announced Listening Parties in 40 cities worldwide, where lucky fans got to hear the full album two weeks before its release.

ROYAL COURT

In our opinion, the best promo "Lord Harry, elf and disco diva of the realm" did for *KISSCO* was a guest appearance on YouTube's *Royal Court* hosted by Brittany Broski in February 2026. Dressed in a crown and cape, with long fake ears, Harry laughed as he discussed the new album, his love of eating "a ridiculous amount of yoghurt every day", a hilarious rendition of Shania Twain's **'Honey, I'm Home'**, and trying not to pee on himself while running marathons. You really have to watch it!

Harry's return at the BRITS 2026 was every fan's dream come true.

100% UNOFFICIAL

"For those who helped me make this. For those who inspire me to make anything. For those who helped me to know when to say NO, when to say YES. For all my friends to dance to."

Harry's album dedication.

So, exactly what is an aperture? It's the opening in a camera lens that controls how much light reaches the sensor. Harry uses the word as a beautiful metaphor for opening yourself up – letting more light, emotion and experience into your life!

TRACK LIST

1. Aperture **2.** American Girls
3. Ready, Steady, Go!
4. Are You Listening Yet?
5. Taste Back
6. The Waiting Game
7. Season 2 Weight Loss
8. Coming Up Roses **9.** Pop
10. Dance No More
11. Paint By Numbers
12. Carla's Song

Together, Together

In January 2026, when Harry announced his *Together, Together* tour, more than 1.3 million tickets sold in mere minutes! It may not be his biggest tour ever, but it is certainly his boldest and bravest ...

THE TOUR THAT'S NOT A TOUR

Unlike his previous *Love On Tour*, *Together, Together* has been described as a 'global residency', with Harry performing 67 shows in just seven cities: Amsterdam, London, São Paulo, Mexico City, New York City, Melbourne and Sydney. Harry wanted to do something different this time around to ensure he could take better care of himself and his band, while also making the shows more environmentally friendly. "I think it will make the shows better," he has said.

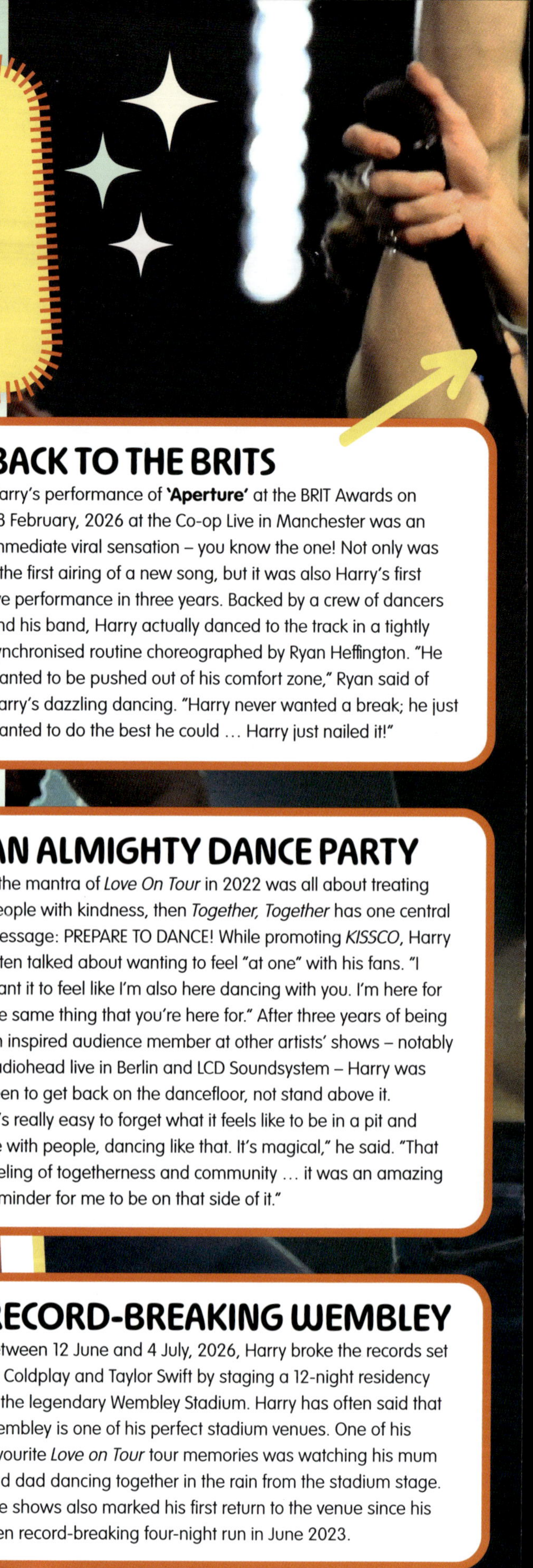

BACK TO THE BRITS

Harry's performance of **'Aperture'** at the BRIT Awards on 28 February, 2026 at the Co-op Live in Manchester was an immediate viral sensation – you know the one! Not only was it the first airing of a new song, but it was also Harry's first live performance in three years. Backed by a crew of dancers and his band, Harry actually danced to the track in a tightly synchronised routine choreographed by Ryan Heffington. "He wanted to be pushed out of his comfort zone," Ryan said of Harry's dazzling dancing. "Harry never wanted a break; he just wanted to do the best he could … Harry just nailed it!"

AN ALMIGHTY DANCE PARTY

If the mantra of *Love On Tour* in 2022 was all about treating people with kindness, then *Together, Together* has one central message: PREPARE TO DANCE! While promoting *KISSCO*, Harry often talked about wanting to feel "at one" with his fans. "I want it to feel like I'm also here dancing with you. I'm here for the same thing that you're here for." After three years of being an inspired audience member at other artists' shows – notably Radiohead live in Berlin and LCD Soundsystem – Harry was keen to get back on the dancefloor, not stand above it. "It's really easy to forget what it feels like to be in a pit and be with people, dancing like that. It's magical," he said. "That feeling of togetherness and community … it was an amazing reminder for me to be on that side of it."

RECORD-BREAKING WEMBLEY

Between 12 June and 4 July, 2026, Harry broke the records set by Coldplay and Taylor Swift by staging a 12-night residency at the legendary Wembley Stadium. Harry has often said that Wembley is one of his perfect stadium venues. One of his favourite *Love on Tour* tour memories was watching his mum and dad dancing together in the rain from the stadium stage. The shows also marked his first return to the venue since his then record-breaking four-night run in June 2023.

BRITS 2026: That iconic viral moment – what a performance!

> We wanna dance with all our friends.
>
> **Harry on Together, Together tour.**

ONE NIGHT ONLY

Put your hands up if you've watched Harry's *One Night Only* Netflix special, filmed at the Co-op Live in Manchester on 6 March, 2026. Harry debuted the new album in full for the "first and only time", plus "some golden oldies" (as he called them!) to nearly 25,000 lucky fans, all of whom secured tickets for just £20 in a lottery. The 90-minute concert was filmed live and then broadcast two days later. The Co-op – a venue that Harry part owns – is located only 45 miles from his teenage home in Cheshire. On the night, Harry told the crowd: "Please sing, dance and by some miracle if you know the words, join in. If you can't have fun, fake it. You might end up on Netflix."

GARDEN STATE OF MIND

On 26 January, 2026, the presale for tickets to see Harry perform at his 30-date residency at Madison Square Garden in New York City – the longest and biggest residency in the venue's history – began. In just one hour, a record-breaking 11.5 million fans tried to get tickets for the 600,000 available seats for shows running between August and October 2026, with support from Jamie xx. Were you one of the lucky ones?

TOGETHER, TOGETHER

For his 2026 UK Wembley Stadium shows, Harry pledged to donate £1 from every ticket sold – with total sales likely to exceed a million tickets! – to the LIVE Trust, a fund that supports small music venues across the country. It means that every fan who buys a ticket is also helping new artists to chase their muscial dreams, just like Harry did.

Harry's Lucky Seven

Let's take a look at the seven lucky cities that Harry has chosen to share the *KISSCO* love with, and the acts he's taking along for the ride ...

NEW YORK

- **Madison Square Garden**
- **Capacity:** 20,000
- **Dates:** 26, 28–29 Aug, 2, 4–5, 9, 11–12, 16, 18–19, 23, 25–26, 30 Sep, 2–3, 7, 9–10, 14, 16–17, 21, 23–24, 28, 30–31 Oct
- **Support:** Jamie xx

Harry has credited Jamie's upbeat electronic music, such as **'I Know There's Gonna Be (Good Times)'**, with helping him with his running. Perhaps you'll catch Harry having a quick jog around the 'Garden during Jamie xx's set?

MEXICO CITY

- **Estadio GNP Seguros**
- **Capacity:** 65,000
- **Dates:** 31 Jul, 1, 4, 7–8 Aug
- **Support:** Jorja Smith

Jorja is a British singer-songwriter who Harry fans might know from her stunning performance of **'As It Was'**, recorded for BBC's Radio 1 *Live Lounge*. Might Mexico City fans be treated to another outing of her gorgeous, slowed-down version?

SÃO PAULO

- **Estadio MorumBIS**
- **Capacity:** 67,000
- **Dates:** 17–18, 21, 24 Jul
- **Support:** Fcukers

Rolling Stone magazine called this super-cool, New York-based electronic band: 'an unstoppable dance-pop duo.' Check out their new song **'I Like It Like That'**, performed recently on *The Tonight Show with Jimmy Fallon*. We know this duo will get the party started in São Paolo.

LONDON

- **Wembley Stadium**
- **Capacity:** 90,000
- **Dates:** 12–13, 17, 19–20, 23, 26–27, 29 Jun, 1, 3–4 Jul
- **Support:** Shania Twain

The Canadian 'Queen of Country-Pop' already wowed Harry fans when they duetted during his 2022 *Coachella* performance. Hands up, who's hoping we get a repeat of Harry and Shania belting out iconic track: **'Man! I Feel Like A Woman!'**?

Harry's a Wembley Stadium Record-Breaker!
"We are incredibly proud to welcome Harry Styles back to Wembley Stadium for what will be a truly historic run of shows. The 12 nights will be among the most special in our stadium's long history."

AMSTERDAM

- **Johan Cruijff Arena**
- **Capacity:** 50,000
- **Dates:** 16–17, 20, 22–23, 26, 29–30 May, 4–5 Jun
- **Support:** Robyn

A pop-icon, famous for her hit **'Dancing On My Own'**. Harry had this to say about the Swedish singer, "I have been a fan of Robyn's since I can remember. As a songwriter and performer, she's undeniable. It is such an honour to have her join me on tour."

12 new songs we can't wait to hear

MELBOURNE

- **Marvel Stadium**
- **Capacity:** 60,000
- **Dates:** 27–28 Nov, 2 Dec
- **Support:** Fousheé

Britanny Fousheé's song, **'Deep End'** went viral for all the right reasons, sampled by artist Sleepy Hallow in 2020. **'Deep End Freestyle'** was a TikTok sensation, with over 320 million streams on Spotify. Fousheé told her Instagram followers she was opening for Harry: "Exciting news!!!! :):)))"

SYDNEY

- **Accor Stadium**
- **Capacity:** 84,000
- **Dates:** 12–13 Dec
- **Support:** Skye Newman

With her impressive vocals and lyrics on hit songs like **'Family Matters'**, Skye caught the ear of Ed Sheeran and Lewis Capaldi, who she opened for in 2025. After supporting Harry for his last shows of the tour in Australia, we think the sky's the limit for this British singer-songwriter.

PICTURE CREDITS

FRONT COVER: PICTURES: Getty Images
4–5 PICTURES: Nancy Kaszerman/ZUMA Press Wire
6–7 PICTURES: Matt Crossick/Empics/Alamy Live News; WENN Rights Ltd; Dominic Lipinski/PA Images; Rw/Media Punch/Alamy Live News; Doug Peters/ STAR MAX/IPx; Imagespace/Alamy Live News; Jordan Strauss/Invision/AP; APA-PictureDesk; Sipa US/Alamy Live News
8–9 WORDS: The Times.com: Harry Lambert / Harry Styles Grammy Speech, 1 February 2026
PICTURES: Starpix/Alexander TUMA; AP Photo/Chris Pizzello
10–11 WORDS: RollingStone.com: Brittany Spanos
PICTURES: Eric Jamison/Invision/AP; WENN Rights Ltd; AP Photo/Chris Pizzello; PA Images/Ian West, TriStar Pictures (This Is Us, 2013)
12–13 WORDS: Another Man Magazine.com: Gemma Styles / ITV: Harry Styles The X Factor Audition broadcast 2010 / 'Another Man Magazine.com: Paul McCartney / One Direction: This Is Us, 2013 / The Jonathan Ross Show: Jonathan Ross, 16 November 2013 / BBC.co.uk/Bitesize / RollingStone.com: Cameron Crowe / Vogue.co.uk: Hamish Bowles
PICTURES: Doug Peters EMPICS Entertainment; Mark Waugh; Brinkstock; WENN Rights Ltd
14–15 WORDS: BBC.co.uk: Colin Paterson / HowardStern.com: Howard Stern / RollingStone.com: Clare Shaffer / RollingStone.com: Rob Sheffield / Rock and Roll Hall of Fame Speech: Harry Styles, 29 March 2019
PICTURES: Pictorial Press Ltd; Michael Wheatley; Gijsbert Hanekroot; Everett Collection Inc; John Angelillo/UPI
16–17 WORDS: RollingStone.com: Cameron Crowe / CBS.com: 'Sunday Morning': Tony Dokoupil 13 October 2017 / / ITV: Harry Styles The X Factor Audition broadcast 2010 / RollingStone.com: Brian Hiatt / Apple Music: Zane Lowe, 17 May 2022 / Dazed and Confused.com: Lynette Nylander
PICTURES: Doug Peters; WENN Rights Ltd; PA Images; Carla Van Wagoner
18–19 WORDS: Billboard.com: Andrew Unterberger / Dazed and Confused.com: Lynette Nylander / Vogue.com: Ella Alexander
PICTURES: Ernie Pollard; Famous/Bang Media International; Cinematic Collection
20–21 WORDS: NPR.com: Mary Louise Kelly & Mallory Yu / EW.com: Amanda Michelle Steiner / i-D.com: Timotheé Chalamet / Eonline.com: Natalie Finn
PICTURES: John Shearer/Invision/AP ; Imagespace/Alamy Live News
22–23 WORDS: RollingStone.com: Cameron Crowe / RollingStone.com: Rolling Stone staff / RollingStone.com: Brittany Spanos / New York Times.com: Joe Coscarelli / Apple Music: Zane Lowe; 'Sign of the Times' music video directed by Yoann Lemoine
PICTURES: Dan Jackman/WENN.com; Rw/Media Punch/Alamy Live News
24–25 WORDS: RollingStone.com: Brian Hiatt
PICTURES: Meleah Loya AFF-USA; AP Photo/Andy Wong; Jeff Wheeler/ Minneapolis Star Tribune/TNS via ZUMA Wire; Scott Garfitt/EMPICS/Alamy Live News
26–27 WORDS: RollingStone.com: Rob Sheffield / Music Week: Ben Homewood / Vogue.com: Hamish Bowles
PICTURES: Scott Garfitt/EMPICS/Alamy Live News; PA Images/Ian West; 'Watermelon Sugar' music video directed by Bradley & Pablo
28–29 WORDS: Harry Styles: Wembley Stadum, 13 June 2023 / Dazed and Confused.com: Lynette Nylander
PICTURES: David Jensen; Famous/Bang Media International; Scott Garfitt/ EMPICS/Alamy Live News
30–31 WORDS: Billboard.com: Associated Press / This Is Us: movie press conference: 19 August 2013 / Access Hollywood: Olivia Wilde, 27 April 2022 / FarOutMagazine.co.uk: Calum Russell / Venice Film Festival Press Conference: 5 September 2022
PICTURES: Paul Treadway; Capital Pictures; Everett Collection Inc/Ron Harvey / Walt Disney Studios Motion Pictures / © Marvel Studios / Courtesy Everett Collection
32–33 WORDS: Vanity Fair.com: Emily Kirkpatrick / TheCut.com: Jenni Miller / RollingStone.com: Rob Sheffield
PICTURES: Christopher Borrelli/Chicago Tribune via ZUMA Press Wire; Matt Crossick/Empics/Alamy Live New
34–35 WORDS: Vogue.com: Hamish Bowles / The Times.com: Harry Lambert / RollingStone.com: EJ Dickson
PICTURES: Kristin Callahan/Everett Collection/Alamy Live News; AFF/Alamy Live News; SIPA US/ Jennifer Graylock; Baden Roth/ZUMA Press Wire; Doug Peters/ STAR MAX/IPx
36–37 WORDS: RollingStone.com: Brittany Spanos
PICTURES: Mr Pics; 'Treat People With Kindness' music video directed by Gabe & Ben Turner; 'Aperture' music video directed by Aube Perrie
38–39 WORDS: BBC Radio One: Nick Grimshaw, 21 February 2013 / Music Week: Ben Homewood / New York Times.com: Joe Coscarelli
PICTURES: WENN Rights Ltd; Matt Crossick/Empics/Alamy Live News
40–41 WORDS: Music Week: Ben Homewood
PICTURES: Matt Crossick/Empics/Alamy Live News; WENN Rights Ltd
42–43 WORDS: Vulture.com: Zoe Haylock
PICTURES: WENN Rights Ltd; 'Watermelon Sugar' music video directed by Bradley & Pablo
44–45 WORDS: Buzzfeed.com: Abha Ahad, 10 April 2022 / RollingStone.com: Brittany Spanos
PICTURES: Doug Peters EMPICS Entertainment; Matt Crossick/Empics/Alamy Live News
46–47 WORDS: bhg.com: Lou Stoppard / BBC.com: Caleb McNeil
PICTURES: Derek Allan/Alamy Live News; AP/ XNY/STAR MAX/IPx; London Entertainment; PA Images/ David Mirzoeff
48–49 WORDS: NPR.com: Leila Fadel / Apple Music: Zane Lowe / RollingStone.com: Rob Sheffield / bhg.com: Lou Stoppard
PICTURES: AP Photo/Chris Pizzello; Pacific Press Media Production Corp./Alamy Live News
50–51 WORDS: Audacy.com: Bru Baker / RollingStone.com: Brittany Spanos / BBC Radio 2: Zoe Ball, 1 April 2022 / Music Week: Ben Homewood
PICTURES: AP Photo/Chris Pizzello; 'As It Was' music video directed by Tanu Muino
52–53 PICTURES: SOPA Images Limited/Alamy Live News; Katrina Young; Wirestock, Inc.; Jordan Strauss/Invision/AP, File
54–55 WORDS: X.com @HarryStyles: 27 February 2013
PICTURES: Matt Crossick/Empics/Alamy Live News; AP Photo/Chris Pizzello; PA Images/Ian West
56–57 WORDS: Another Man Magazine.com: Gemma Styles / Instagram.com @hshq: 23 July 2020 / RollingStone.com: Cameron Crowe / Digital Spy.com: Kate Goodacre / This Is Us, 2013 (directed by Morgan Spurlock).
PICTURES: Fred Duval; AP Photo/Jae C. Hong; Jamie Lamor Thompson; TriStar Pictures/Photo12; Kathy Hutchins; Vianney Le Caer/Invision/AP
58–59 WORDS: RollingStone.com: Brittany Spanos / Guardian.co.uk: Tom Lamont / RollingStone.com: Brittany Spanos & Amy X. Wang
PICTURES: John Angelillo/UPI; Kathy Hutchins; Lev Radin; Cinematic Collection; Roger Southwell
60–61 WORDS: SiriusXM: Howard Stern, 4 March 2020
PICTURES: Billy Bennight/ZUMA Press Wire; PA Images/Ian West
62–63 WORDS: Billboard.com: Hannah Dailey / The Times.com: Harry Lambert / GQ.com: Jonathan Heaf
PICTURES: WENN Rights Ltd; John Angelillo/UPI; PA Images/Ian West; SIPA US/ Anthony Behar; APA-PictureDesk
64–65 WORDS: RunnersWorld.com: Sophie Heawood / BBC Radio One: Greg James, 23 January 2026 / Royal Court: Brittany Broski, 25 February 2026
PICTURES: IMAGO/Steve Vas; 'Aperture' music video directed by Aube Perrie
66–67 WORDS: Apple Music: Zane Lowe, 4 March 2026 / TheTimes.com: Roisin Kelly / CapitalFM: Jordan North, 26 January 2026 / Instagram.com @hshq, 22 February 2026
PICTURES: Matt Crossick/Empics/Alamy Live News; Sipa US/Alamy Live News
68–69 WORDS: TheFace.com: Shaad D'Souza / Instagram.com @foushee, January 2026
PICTURES: Ben Houdijk; Ben Adams/Sipa USA; iStock/ Cristian Lourenço; Shutterstock/ Christian Bertrand; Shutterstock/ Pim Kraster; Wirestock Creators; Lev Radin; imageSPACE via ZUMA Press Wire; Steve Vas/Geisler-Fotopress; Shutterstock/ Aija Lehtonen; Shutterstock/ Wirestock Creators; Shutterstock/ Gerry H; Shutterstock/ red3108; The Fcukers appeared on The Tonight Show Starring Jimmy Fallon, March 3, 2026